Donald H. Tippett.

Christ Church

Denver

1925

A SMALL TOWN MAN

A SMALL TOWN MAN

BY
MARY AUSTIN

HARPER & BROTHERS PUBLISHERS
NEW YORK AND LONDON

A Small Town Man

E-Z

AUTHOR'S PREFACE

In March of 1915, when the original manuscript was first presented to the publishers, it bore the title of *A Small Town Man* under which it is now reissued. But, on the ground that such a title would be so little appreciated by the public as to prejudice them against the material of the book, the publishers so strongly, and perhaps wisely, advised against its use that the author was constrained to agree with them. Accordingly, the first edition, as well as the serial publication of the story in the *North American Review*, appeared under the caption *The Man Jesus*.

There was also in that first edition something which has been a sore point of conscience with the author ever since. That was a final chapter in which the author's conclusion about the man was held in abeyance, and an attempt made to suggest what were believed to be the lasting values of the Life, by an interpretation of the less important teachings. At that time it was thought by my advisers that the very terms of mysticism and genius were so little understood by American readers, that the point of my real conclusions would be entirely missed. In this I concurred, but with the reservation that, if at any time in the future I felt that an estimate of Jesus as a mystic would be appreciated, the book was to be revised and re-issued. Both author and publisher now agreeing that a more general familiarity with the terms and scope of mysticism, will warrant a restatement of the claims of Jesus to be considered, although a small-town man, the greatest of mystics, this new edition has been undertaken.

It was at Rome, in the summer of 1907, that I began to be interested in the man, Jesus, since it was there that I first realized how completely we had lost him. I had gone directly to Italy from a hot, tawny land, where shepherds watched their flocks, where the fields were watered by led streams and the hills terraced with vines and olives. I had lived in small towns and smaller, had known dark peoples whose wisdom was all of the inner understanding, among whom prophets and natural leaders were of normal occurrence. And I had counted on that background, so like to the one to which Jesus was native, to put me directly in the way which I sup-posed would lead back from the Church of Rome to the man in whose name it was established. But what I found at Rome was so alien to my expectations that, without the starred references in the guide books, I wouldn't have identified it.

Jesus was not there for me in Roman art, as the

fifteenth century had painted him; in death so de-
plorable, in life so wan and womanish, so *elegant;*
nor was he anywhere to be discovered in the pomp
of ritual nor the bemused, Greco-Roman mysticism
of worship. So then and there in the catacombs, in
the library of the Vatican, and later in other great
libraries, wherever there were original texts and con-
firming material, I began to look for the plain man
who was the vehicle of his revelation. I looked for
him by the one method in the technique of which I
had some mastery, the method of the folklorist, with
precisely the same frame of mind in which I approached any other collection of hero tales. Here, I
said, was a man who produced an impression on his
own and succeeding ages such as no man else has left,
a small-town man, whose life and sayings are reported
by his fellow-townsmen. In this material I should be
much at home.

It will readily be seen that the item about Jesus
which furnishes the title of this revised edition, is also
the one which affords the closest point of contact for
the average modern, himself a small-towner, with
this transcendent personality. In personally announcing it, the author has been interested to find it
met, on the part of small-town people, with a rising
Ah! of illumination, and on the part of the incor-
rigibly urban with an *Oh!* of half dismay, so true
do all our concepts of Jesus run to our personal bias.

So, in the very act of putting forth the title, *A Small Town Man* has become a symbol to the author, as is hoped it will be to the reader, of the one universal strain of alikeness, differing only in expression, among all peoples, the alikeness of the mystical, inknowing faculty which reached its highest expression in Jesus. It is also the happiest augury of a possibility of a finally unified human race, since, once a generally comprehensible vocabulary of terms is accepted, the mystics themselves are all agreed that this is the one field of human activity in which neither race, nor privilege, nor the quality of preferred intellectuation, can affect the findings; the field of inknowing, spiritual perception.

It was not with any expectation of writing a book that the seven years of scholarly research which lie behind *A Small Town Man* were begun. For the first four or five years the motivation was purely that of personal illumination.

By the end of that time certain strongly marked outlines of the Life began to appear:—that Jesus was a small-town mystic, that he had a genius for mysticism; that his teaching, instead of being extended over three years as is commonly supposed, was of little more than a year's duration; and finally that the accounts of his post-crucifixion reappearances were, by every test of the folklorist, true, and not excessively legendized accounts of a man believed to have been legally executed, discovered to be alive, showing himself to a few intimates under conditions calculated to protect himself and them from further conflict with the authorities. Upon this outline, beginning with the nine credible sayings, bit by bit, by the same method in which authentic history is being recovered from our aboriginal myths, the figure of Jesus as here presented, was built up.

On the fifth day of January, 1915, I threw away my notes and began to write. About the middle of March immediately following, the manuscript of the first edition was ready for the publisher.

If I recall these details now, having formerly omitted all reference to source and processes, it is not without intention. The same intention that led me, from the beginning, to decline all the patter of professional scholarship, all its working signs of citation and attribution, the tithings of the mint and cumin of evidence. These things I have always recognized as the male ritual of truth-seeking, the castings away of the staff and the shoes of the sincere man on his way to the burning bush within which is God. It is only by these successive freeings of himself from prepossessions and prejudices that the intellectual man can approach truth with any approximation. For the average male soul exists at the focus, perhaps simultaneously at the foci, of a vortex of the unorganized stuff of personality beside which the more completely centralized soul of woman has always appeared a prolific source of mystification. Thus man moves outward toward the ordered conclusion, separating himself from what was originally other men's, by identifying and shucking from his soul the serialization of himself which it is his natural life process to produce. Thus it has become the supreme courtesy of male scholarship to trail all the litter of the workshop after him in the shape of footnotes and cross references and appendices. But a woman is under no such obligation. There is no place in which she is as much at home as in the midst of the bush at whose burning she would not hesitate to boil the family kettle. The only obligation that she recognizes is that whatever is brought forth must, with whatever pains, be brought forth alive. If necessary she dies that this may be accomplished. And her natural method with whatever she produces is the method of gestation.

The only sure way, then, of giving to the woman's contribution its full evaluation, is for her to be faithful to her own pattern, of which vital organization rather than explication is the criterion. Otherwise, she produces little besides a lifeless imitation of the works of men. Believing this, I should hold myself faithless to my gift of courage, and to whatever grace I have, to present my work in any other fashion than

woman fashion, even though I be proved in the end
to have overlooked, or even faultily recalled, some
of the minutiæ of scholarship. Liking, as little as
anybody, to be found at fault, I take that risk;
realizing that I am by no means past the mischance,
from which I have suffered much, practically, in the
past, of finding my work discredited or at least under-
valued by the male mind. It is perhaps not realized
even by men, who hold all the approaches of that
perilous passage a book must run on its way to its
public, to what extent a woman's book is put to the
man question. For there are men so sincerely of the
opinion that a book which has not a certain foot foremost, such a touching of the forelock of learning,
such gestures, so distributed, two steps to the left
and one to the right, is not really a book at all, that
they have never asked themselves how that came
to be the accepted notion of a book. But if I am not
past the possibility of having my life of Jesus neglected because shorn of the male convention of
scholarship, I was, even in 1915, past being daunted
by it.

The only other note I could add to this preface to
the second and last edition would be my reason for
writing at all about a two-thousand-year-old revelation. That is because it was only after having
unwound my own life from the coil of a pattern laid
upon it by the story of Jesus, exteriorized by the

succeeding generations of his followers, that I saw how bindingly that pattern has rested on our life, our art, upon the very prepossession in which the creative life is lived among us. This was not so clear in 1915 as it is to-day, now that the shape of that pattern is dissolving; so much clearer now that it is enough, perhaps, to say that that I have written this whole book for the sake of its last sentence.

M. A.

A SMALL TOWN MAN

Moses commanded us a law, even the inheritance of the congregation of Jacob.—Deut. xxxiii, 4.

[The above was taught to every Hebrew child by his father as soon as the child was old enough to speak. A little later he was taught the first part of the Shema, which follows. The whole Shema, including Deut. ix, 13-21, and Num. xv, 37-41, was recited by every devout Hebrew morning and night.]

Hear, O Israel, the Lord our God is One Lord:—
And thou shalt love the Lord thy God with all thine heart and with all thy soul and with all thy might. And these words, which I command thee this day, shall be in thine heart: and thou shalt teach them diligently to thy children, and thou shalt talk of them when thou sittest in thine house, and when thou walkest by the way, and when thou liest down and when thou risest up. And thou shalt bind them for a sign upon thine hand, and they shall be as a frontlet between thine eyes. And thou shalt write them upon the posts of thy house, and on thy gates.—Deut. vi, 4-9.

A SMALL TOWN MAN

I

WHEN Tiberius Cæsar had been some fifteen
years upon the seat of Roman Empire there
arose, in an inconsiderable quarter of his realm, a
man of a destiny so tragic and a character so com-
manding that a score of centuries have scarcely
served to dim the appeal of his unique personality.
He arose upon the Bridge of the World, shaken as it
was with the passing of Roman power between
Egypt and Asia, among the people whose voice
among the nations was as the voice of one crying
small wares in the midst of traffic. They were the
Keepers of the Bridge. Their race had been born
amid its ribs and buttresses; they had been swept
from it by Egypt and Assyria, whence, after generations of captivity, they had found their way
back to it with the instinct of homing-pigeons. They
sat upon the Bridge between the desert and the sea
and trafficked with the nations going past; they

trafficked even for the right to sit and traffic in their
ancient seats. Sometimes they fought for it, but that
was only when they were threatened in their sole
other distinction.   For they were not only a race of
traffickers; they dreamed greatly.

When the bazars were shut and the smoke of the
evening sacrifice gone up, they forgathered upon the
housetops with their feet tucked under them and
dreamed a splendid and orderly heaven with Him of
the Ineffable Name sitting in the midst of the vault,
surrounded by rank on rank of Seraphim and
Cherubim, angels and archangels, all singing and with
flaming wings.   They went further and dreamed a
world of men in the same order and symmetry, a
world dripping with milk and honey where there
should be none hurt and none crying any more, and
the lion and the lamb lying down together.   It was
perhaps a shopkeeper's heaven, with everything
ticketed and tucked away in it—think of a people
undertaking to name the whole heavenly host!—but
it surpassed in grandeur, in singleness of conception,
the hybrid theogonies of the pagan world as much
as the Græco-Roman Zeus-Pater, the Thunderer,
was surpassed by their *High and Holy One Who
Inhabiteth Eternity*.

And for the right to worship this One-God in their
own fashion and to keep undefiled His holy places the
Jews would fight on occasion, but it was the only

thing they would fight for. Their two great national
achievements—the winning forth from Egypt and
the return from captivity—they owed not to the
sword, but to that quality which has made them
before all others a business people. Once religious
freedom was assured to them, they made what
terms they could for a degree of political inde-
pendence.

These are two things to remember about the Jews
in thinking of the man who arose among them: that
their dreaming was all of God, and that when there
was anything of great import to be done they thought
of every other way to go about it rather than by
fighting. It is well to keep these in mind because,
however much a man of any race may seem to
oppose the genius of the tribe that produced him,
it is impossible that he should not take from them
in some fashion the line of his direction. The
third item in the resolution of the external forces
that determined the mold of the man Jesus, was
the fact that he was sprung from a mountain
people.

That was a country split into shoulders and
summits, into narrow, knife-cut valleys and flowering
oases between high, tumbled barrens. It followed
that the inhabitants were divided into tribes and
half tribes, and these into factions. It is always so
in mountain countries where field is separated from

field by waste, and village is buttressed against village. Carmel has its foot in the sea, Lebanon is cut off, Hermon the white-haired stands up over Naphtali, Gilead and Ephraim are divided. The Samaritans were despised by the Judeans, who found the Galileans crude; and the Galileans themselves doubted if any good thing could come out of Nazareth. When they needed, therefore, a common bond they did not find it, as other tribes are prone to do, in political advantage or identity of material interests; they found it in the common dream, in the reality of a common spiritual experience. They fought for Jehovah and the holy places, even though they could not agree among themselves which places were the holiest. That was how it happened that the people who never achieved anything like national integrity for themselves, except for the briefest periods, were the first to effect a movement toward the universal state. For when their great man came, he walked, though they failed for the time to appreciate it, in the deep-rutted track which Hebrew thought had made for him.

The first that was heard of him was in connection with one of those singular characters which seem to have arisen from time to time among all ancient peoples, a true prophet by all the marks, of the stripe of Malachi and Habakkuk and Jeremiah.

This John, called the Baptist, out of the hills of

Judea, but citizen of that portion of the Bridge which reached from the roots of Lebanon past Naphtali, past Tabor and Hermon, past the plain of Esdraelon stretching to the narrow Phœnician coast, down the Rift of Jordan to the dead, desert sea. For this assumption we have the natural temper of his mind and the fact that he was amenable to the civil authority of Herod, Tetrarch of Galilee. He took a true prophet's liberty with his sovereign by telling him exactly what he thought of him, and Herod, for his part, accorded John the customary recognition of kings to prophets by shutting him up in prison and finally making an end of him. But before that much had happened.

About the time that the shadow of madness began to grow upon the mind of Tiberius Claudius Nero and the hateful race of informers fattened under the hand of Sejanus, when Herod Antipas was living openly with his brother's wife, and Aretas, father of his legal consort, breathing war against him, this John began suddenly to preach the kingdom of heaven at hand. To the orthodox Jew the phrase, Kingdom of Heaven, meant the specific realization of the great national dream, an institution so Hebraic in its scope and limitation that it was doubtful if the world at large had any place in it beyond a vague consignment to an outer circle of darkness where there was wailing and gnashing of teeth.

Therefore when John began to proclaim its immanence and declare it in that high impassioned style
which is the hall-mark of prophetic inspiration, the
little world of Jewry went out to hear him.

In the first place, it might be true; and in the
second, John was, on the whole, very good entertainment. He was an ascetic dressed in a garment
of camel's-hair girt about with skins, living off the
land, on seeds of sparse-grown desert shrubs and
honey from the hiving rocks along the bluffs of
Jordan. Then there was this interesting new ritual
of baptism — that was a poor Jew indeed, who
couldn't make room in his life for *one* more ceremonial—and he had a lively condemnation for such
as are in authority, which is always pleasing to those
not themselves among the authorities. Also there
were devout souls who were in expectation, looking
for the great day of Israel. Among them was the
man from Nazareth.

He must have come on foot from his home, a day's
journey, down the deepest rift in the world—it is
not for mere poetizing that the river is called Jordan,
the Down-comer—to the ford where Naaman washed,
where the Ark of the Covenant passed over and
the reeds are still shaken in the wind out of Haran.
The soil hereabout is as red as a red heifer, streaked
with marl. The river comes down between ribbons
of deep poisonous green in a jungle of tamarisk and

oleander. Westward Judea lifts by terraces, dim under the heat haze, scarred by volcanic waste; east away lie the level tops of Gilead, out of which the prophet Elijah had so mysteriously burst upon the times of Ahab. Many thoughts of Israel past and future must have flocked with the crowds that went out to John's preaching in the shut valley of the Jordan. Crowds there must have been far beyond what is indicated by the meager report, for the prophet succeeded not only in attracting the attention of the reigning house, but in staving off his end for a year or two by reason of his popularity. But for his survival in history and in the world beyond the Bridge he was debtor to the man from Nazareth.

Of this man, up to the moment of his contact with John and the reorganization of his spiritual forces which took place immediately afterward, very little is known. His very name of Joshua has come down to us only in the Greek form of Jesus. Beyond that we have the mere mention of his parents, Joseph and Mary, brothers James and Jude, Simon and Joses, and unnamed sisters. There is a tradition that he was born in Bethlehem while his mother was on a journey, all of which is set down with great circumstantiality by one Luke, a physician writing about the middle of the first century; but, if true, Jesus never referred to the place and never revisited

it.   He was brought up in the hill town of Nazareth
to his father's trade of carpenter.   This much seems
certain.   For the rest we have a great body of
legend such as collects readily about any man of
singular gift or destiny.   These in their place should
be examined; for the light they throw on the way
in which, within a generation after his death, he
came to be regarded, they have much to commend
them.   But of plain fact there is this precisely: a
young Jew, something under thirty, of the better
class of working-men, by name, Joshua Ben Joseph,
receiving the rite of baptism from a wild anchorite
on the mud-banks of a muddy river.

There had been preaching first, perhaps a psalm-
singing.   It would have been in the nature of a
pilgrimage, this exodus from Jerusalem; from Samaria, from the parts of Galilee and the east-lying
Græco-Syrian Decapolis to hear the prophet.   It was
a time when men looked every way for salvation.
John they heard with an instinctive attempt to
connect him with their past, with those of his own
trade prophecy.   It was so they could best judge
what his teaching might mean to the future of Israel.
In their dreams the Jews looked for a Messiah,
but in their hearts they expected Elijah, greatest
of all True-Speaking.   Among the faithful to this
day is not the door left open on the Paschal evening
for the return of the prophet?   It was hereabout

that he was last seen of men, parting the Jordan with his garment, passing over dry-shod before he was taken up. . . . (*Oh, the chariots of Israel and the horsemen thereof!*") Memories like this prompted inquiry.

"Who art thou, then?" No doubt as they waited a supernatural thrill went over them. It was a time and a place when almost anything might happen. But John had an answer for them.

"The voice of one crying in the Wilderness. Prepare ye the way of the Lord!" So now, they knew him. He was the forerunner. This also was according to scripture. But there was more of John's message, and that astonishing.

Of old time the prophets had preached to kings and high priests, to the nation in its entirety, rebuking tyrannies and putting down false gods, restoring alike the altars and the ancient liberties. The new note that came in with John was the note of personal repentance, and not that only, but fruit meet for repentance brought forth on every bough, "For the axe is laid to the root of the trees: therefore every tree which bringeth not forth fruit shall be hewn down and cast into the fire." Judge how this was received by the Hebrew who counted himself safe in being of the stock of Abraham. "And think not," John warned them, "to say within yourselves, We have Abraham to our father, for

I say unto you that God is able of these stones to raise up children unto Abraham."

This was the astonishment and the affront of John's preaching. The Kingdom was at hand, and being a Jew wasn't of itself sufficient to get you into it. It seems certain that many of his hearers, among them Herod, rejected such doctrine. But Herod John reproved openly for his adulteries, and to the Pharisees and Sadducees when he saw them come to his baptism he scoffed, "O ye generations of vipers, who hath warned *you* to flee from the wrath to come?"

You perceive here the ancient prophetic touch both in the temper of his mind and the imagery. It would have been the end of the dry season, and all along the heights of Gilead quick fires ran in the stubble. In his mind's eye John saw the tribes of formalists and hypocrites like swarms of vipers and scorpions scuttling for safety before the fires unquenchable. But for the common people who came asking sincerely what they should do, John had another answer, "He that hath two coats let him impart to him who hath none, and he that hath food let him do likewise." To the publicans he advised, "Exact no more than that which is appointed to you"; and to the soldiers, "Do violence to no man, neither exact anything wrongly, and be content with your wages."

An all too brief report, but explicit. In that last clause is swept away every possibility of supposing that John came to head a revolt against the power of Rome or to reconstruct the social order. This is important in connection with what happened afterward, for the teaching of the Baptist is the sole personal influence that can be traced in the work of the man from Nazareth. Words, phrases of the Forerunner, cropped up again in his ministry; its opening slogan was the same call to repentance. On the death of its founder the first definite movement of the Christian organization was in the direction of John's program—they had all things in common; he that had two coats imparted to him that had none, and he that had food did likewise. Whether the disciples owed it most to Jesus or to John, it marks for the two men a common source of inspiration, a common expectation.

The message of the Baptist was the thread by which Jesus felt his way to the heart of his own mission. The kingdom was at hand, it was to be prepared for, but the preparation had not all to do with God and man; it was bound up somehow with the relations between man and his neighbor. All this could hardly have come of one preaching. Years afterward Paul found Apollos, an Alexandrine convert, spreading the baptism of John as far afield as Ephesus. All of which goes to show the pertinence of his doctrine and the man's grip on his audience.

Of this there were both numbers and variety. The river here meets the highways; legionaries went by between Petra and Damascus, caravans from Egypt to the parts of Arabia. At the ford the thick ribbon of tamarisk and oleander called the Pride of Jordan is set back by the canebrake. Old herons go a-fishing there; the hot air of the Rift is filled with the pestiferous hum of flies. By day there would be the noise of the caravans and the purr of the sleek water; by night the friendly pilgrim camps, the brush fires of the wood-cutters; at times the roar of a lion in the jungle, and the snorting of the tethered asses. Over all the voice of the prophet prevailing.

"Repent ye, repent ye, for the Kingdom of Heaven is at hand . . . but one mightier than I cometh, the latchet of whose shoes I am not worthy to unloose, whose fan is in his hand, and he will thoroughly purge his floor and will gather the wheat unto his garner, but the chaff he will burn with a fire unquenchable.

"I have baptized you with water, but he shall baptize you with fire and the holy spirit."

Among those who, hearing, went down to receive the rite of cleansing was the young man from Nazareth; as he went he felt the heavens opened and the Spirit of God descend upon him; and as it were a voice saying, "This is my beloved son in whom I am well pleased."

§

All the God-tales come straight out of the heart of man; all the devil-tales also.

There is a part of us which lies remote from the region of material sense, open to all manner of undetermined influences. We are torn by these things, exalted, cast down, informed, and illumined to a degree surpassing what comes to us through the conscious intelligence. But when we speak of them it can only be in terms shaped for us by the latest guess at the nature of the disturbance, God, demon, or the spirits of ancestors. The young man from Nazareth, as he passed under the Baptist's hand through the water of baptism, knew what sounded in his soul for the voice of God the Father. He was led by it up out of the Rift of Jordan into the Wilderness. But of all that happened to him there we know no more than can be conveyed in a tale he made of it, a kind of allegory of the soul's immaterial conflict in terms of devil and angels.

It was so in those days men spoke to one another of experiences that passed below the threshold of exterior sense. Doubtless when he told it, it was so understood, as a thing experienced rather than seen. Not for hundreds of years did the story of the temptation put on the gross materiality under which the Middle Ages knew it.

That it was his most significant experience we gather from the fact that it was the only thing that ever happened to Jesus which he thought worth speaking about. That he spoke of this with such particularity as to impress it on all his disciples is our warrant for believing that nothing else out of the ordinary ever had happened to him. What he saw, what he lived through, what he heard talked about as a carpenter at Nazareth was so undistinguished a part of the community experience that we are free to restore it from the copious researches of scholarship. Behind this thin veil of parable we have his own account of the essential elements of his genius.

Here then is the story of the carpenter in the Wilderness as he told it. After he had heard sounding through all his soul the acknowledgment of his sonship, himself part and parcel of the divine being, he went up and out of the Ghor into the Wilderness of Judea between the brook Cherith and the vineyards of Engedi, a terrible blank land, treeless, spined with low shrubs from under which the adder starts. He was around and about in it forty days fasting. He saw vultures sailing and the blue wall of Moab through the mist of evaporation from the great salt sea—"smoke going up for ever"—all opalescent in the unclouded light, but saw no man. He laid himself open to the sense the desert gives of being possessed, of begin held and occupied by personality and power. Forty days and nights the spirit led and eluded him, and at last he grappled with it. Then said the tempter, Jesus being faint with hunger, "If thou be the son of God command that these stones be made bread." And again, seeing he got nothing by that method, the devil set him on a high place, as it were the pinnacle of the temple, and bade him cast himself down, since if he were the true son of God the angels should have charge over him, lest he so much as dash his foot against a stone. Finally from a high mountain the devil showed him the kingdoms of this world and the glory of them, saying, "All these things will I give if thou wilt fall down and worship me."

Answering out of the deep wells of scripture, the man from Nazareth answered his own soul.

He had gone into the desert a carpenter with the word of John in his ears and the call of God in his consciousness; he came out of it prophet and teacher. To know the full force in his life of the answer he found to the questing Spirit, we must know what went in with him other than John's doctrine. I do not mean what schooling, what human experiences, what things observed and noted among men, for of these he had no more than was common to scores of other young men who went down to John's baptism. It was none of these things which enabled him to clear himself at the stroke of revelation from the old Hebrew notion of man apart from God as the sheep are apart from the shepherd, of another nature and kind from him. For Israel thought of God as a sheep thinks of a shepherd. One who led by green pastures, fed, fended, or destroyed as He thought good for them. But Jesus, from the first we hear of him, comes filled with the sense of divine kinship, possessed of it as a son is possessed of the attributes of a father—an idea so germane to us now that we can scarcely realize with what effect of the heavens being opened it burst upon him.

It was not, then, any question of the relationship between himself and God that drove him to the Wilderness. There is something still to seek for the clear understanding of the parable of the Temptations;—*Something* there was between Jesus and John, something between Jesus and his disciples, which was either so well understood as to require no explanation or so profoundly felt that it lay beyond the reach of expression. I find it in the one feature of the Hebrew religion which distinguishes it from all its contemporaries;—in the conviction of the reality of righteousness.

The cult of Jehovah had outlived on its own

ground the gods of Ninevah and Tyre, of Egypt and Babylon; it maintained itself in the face of dying Græco-Romanism by that one article of its faith which was never lost sight of even in its worst apostasy—namely, that ethical rightness is no mere matter of opinion, but a living principle. The pagan had no use whatever of his gods except in what they could do for him; he never, so to speak, knew exactly where to have them. In some fashion he recognized an essential element in Things, dung-heaps, orchards, fevers—which, if he could but put himself in harmony with it, could be "worked."

When it could no longer be worked in his favor he got him a new god amenable to another sort of persuasion. But Jehovah was the god of Israel conquering or Israel conquered. This point toward which we struggle so slowly with all our science, our knowledge of heredity, and the constitution of human society, was the common possession of Jesus and his people; the revelation of righteousness as a thing to be eternally sought after, whether one lost or won by it.

This, then, was what lies behind and renders intelligible the fragments of scripture with which Jesus met the importunities of his personal life, coming to him in the form of the arch-tempter on the mount of the Wilderness.

In the first and second of these we have a direct
answer to two of the most vexed and mistaken
problems of his name people. To the suggestion
that he should appease the desires of his man-nature
by causing stones to be made bread, Jesus had answered that man does not live by bread alone, but
by every word which proceedeth out of the mouth
of God. It is impossible to think of this as presenting itself to the man from Nazareth as a personal
problem only—the problem of youth with its hungry desires for food, a mate, houses, trappings.
But whether settled for himself or humanity, the
question was never reopened. This is no story of
a plain man finding himself, but of a soul unselfed
from the beginning, apprised of his power, sure of
his high calling, seeking behind all material lack,
the essential disharmony which his message was to
heal. Socially minded as he showed himself to be,
he must have faced here and struck out of his own
course the futility of attempting to achieve the
kingdom by the relief of immediate social discom-
fort. Hungry as his time was, sore with poverty
and injustice and oppression, when he went back to
it, it was not with any palliative, but with the keen
sword of the spirit. The misery of his world rose
up against him, assailed him through his great gift
of compassion, threatened to engulf him; but always we see him striking clear of it, committing

himself to the Word with such confidence as a bird commits itself to the air or a great fish to the deep.

But if Jesus rejected the principle of direct relief as a means of bringing the kingdom to pass, he was even more explicit in his condemnation of direct political action as establishing it. For the devil in Jesus' time was no mere hoof-and-tail bogy, but that Lucifer whose seat was once in heaven. And what else can the worship of him mean in connection with the kingdoms of this world and the power and glory of them, than the use of satanic means, political intrigue, jealousy, faction, conspiracy, by means of which the rebellious angels fell? We shall come closer than this to the mind of Jesus touching the social organization, but we shall get nothing more decisive than his, "Get thee behind me!"

For the second item of the adventure of a soul in the Wilderness there can be no interpretation possible except we begin with what sooner or later must be allowed to Jesus, that he was a mystic. In saying this no more is implied than is true in some degree of every one of us. It is to say that the larger half of him lay consciously in the region of which we have already had occasion to speak, the unmapped region of the subconsciousness. Your true mystic is one who lives at home in that country to which most of us repair infrequently on a visit, or are snatched by compelling incidents of passion or suffering. The notion that mysticism savors somehow of impracticality leads us to deny its existence in ourselves, which amounts to a denial that there is anything in us which is immaterial or uncomprehended. To such as these it is a surprise to know that the states of mysticism preserve an orderly sequence and are accompanied by definite gains and powers. Such powers the man from Nazareth attained. To have endured this particular temptation he must already have been aware of them when he went up out of Jordan.

Almost the first we hear of Jesus on his return to Galilee, was as a healer of men's bodies and a reader of their minds. Such powers cannot be thought of as coming leaping to the demand; they are acquired by pains and labor. If, then, we concede that when Jesus went into the Wilderness he knew himself possessed of such capabilities, we have in the incident of the pinnacle from which he was to cast himself down, a symbol of the peculiar temptation of the gifted. To make himself safe, to make himself wondered at, set apart, this is the devil's bait for the saint and the adept. Whether or not this was what Jesus implied in his personal narrative, it is borne out by his whole attitude toward his special capacities. All through his career he displayed, in the use of his extraordinary gifts, a reticence and sense of proportion unequaled among men of genius.

This was the fruit of the Wilderness, the subordination of bodily and material needs to the spiritual, based on the perception of the spiritual as the only reality; the consecration of gifts to service rather than to personal aggrandizement; the rejection of political action as a means of attaining the desired social equilibrium. If this were not the implicit meaning of the parable it was at least a thing achieved within the scope of his personality. Throughout the remainder of his life he is plainly seen so to direct his own operations. For in this he excelled all the saints, in his spiritual efficiency. What he had determined on the mountain he went forth to preach in Galilee.

With great love hast thou loved us,
  O Lord our God.
And with much overflowing pity hast thou pitied
 us,
  Our father and our king.
For the sake of our fathers who trusted in thee,
 and thou taughtest them the statutes of life,
  Have mercy upon us!
Enlighten our eyes in the law;
 cause our hearts to cleave to thy commandments;
 unite our hearts to love and fear thy name;
 and we shall not be put to shame.
  World without end.
For thou art a God who preparest salvation;
 and thou hast chosen us from among all nations
 and tongues;
 and hast in truth brought us nearer to thy great
 name.
  Selah!
That we may lovingly praise thee and thy unity.
Blessed be the Lord who in love chose his people
 Israel!

[A prayer which was part of the synagogue service during the time of Jesus.]

II

OF this Herod against whom John inveighed we shall see enough to warrant some description. A Jew by religion, Greek in culture, though with a touch of Semitic magnificence, Roman by affiliation; handsome, undisciplined, perfumed, wily, he no doubt deserved the epithet of Fox, which the man of Nazareth afterward applied to him. Fearing Rome a little and his constituents as much as rulers of the Jews have always feared them, he nevertheless claims a greater share of our attention than either of the other sons of Herod the Great, among whom his kingdom was divided.

Archelaus, Ethnarch of Idumea, Judea and Samaria, came into direct conflict with the Sanhedrin at Jerusalem, was worsted by them, deposed and superseded by a procurator under the hand of the Emperor. Philip on the north, touching the borders of Galilee, loved peace and got it, and got nothing else; but if Herod, called Antipas, Tetrarch of Galilee, were judged less objectionable than his father, it was because his restricted field gave him fewer opportunities for getting himself disliked.

Of those that he had it cannot be said that he neglected any of them.

On the present occasion he was discovering himself in the irritating position of a man who has flouted society and the gods on the grounds of a justifying passion, and finds that neither the gods nor society has accepted his justification. During a recent visit to Rome he had become enamoured of his brother's wife, whom he had brought away with him; whereupon Aretas, King of Arabia, father of his legal consort, assaulted his southern border. It was while his affairs were at this pass that John arose, shaking out the banner of prophetic denunciation.

Evidently those who accepted his moral conclusions judged John competent to deal with the situation. The man from Nazareth, though made one of John's adherents by the rite of baptism, passed to his own country without any attempt to support the Baptist's attack upon existing conditions. If from the mount of temptation he had seen the thin line of the legionaries fumbling the dry passes of the Arabian border, or at the ford of Jordan detachments going down from the garrison at Capernaum to eke out the Tetrarch's slender resources, it waked in him no impulse of resistance to the established order. Wrapt still in his personal revelation, he came up out of the Rift into Galilee.

From the hills of Nazareth one sees the ships of
the Empire low like a flock of gulls on the rim of
the Mediterranean; below him the oleanders are
pink against the whitewashed walls, and blunt,
dark oaks overhang the strips of tillage. A little town, a butt, a Jack Dullard of a town among
the smart new cities of Tiberias and Capernaum
with their Greek theaters and Roman garrisons;
a little, old, shave-head, bewigged Hebrew housewife of a town, to judge by the proverb, which
suckled a prophet and did not know him. But
at Capernaum converged all the roads that went
over the Bridge: new Roman roads, Phœnician
coast roads, the oldest roads in the world between
Egypt and Asia; and the traffic of the world went
by on them. Herod rebuilt Tiberias and had a
palace there; he fortified Sepphoris; village touched
village. Here, as to a theater more befitting his
mission than hill-bent Nazareth, Jesus moved,
new-born from the Wilderness. It is believed he
had a house there, but of a shop and the appurte-
nances of his trade there is no mention.

On omissions slight as this, a world sick with the
sloth of the Middle Ages made of him a kind of
respectable mendicant. One finds him, however,
going about with other householders, decent folk
owning their own business, employing hired servants,
paying their own scores, and obliged to ask no man's

leave if they chose to lay aside their work for a season to go a-proselyting. It is of record that the Emperor Domitian, having accepted the Davidic descent for the family of Nazareth, sent for what remained of them, fearful lest they set up a belated claim of royalty. There were brought to him two grandsons of Jude, the brother of Jesus, who showed him the callouses of their hands and confessed to owning about forty acres of land, from which they made their living and the taxes. Does the possession of that forty acres in any way account for the freedom with which the brother of Jude drew upon the sowing and the reaping, the wine-press and the orchard, for the figure of the Kingdom? He drew, in fact, far less on his own trade and his father's. Too much has been made of his being a carpenter—every good Jew taught his son a trade; Paul was a tent-maker, and *he* stood before kings and was versed in pagan philosophies.

Nor was there anything in the conditions in Galilee at the time from which to draw the pathetic figure of poverty. Galilee of the Gentiles was a great hostelry; trade flourished, olive-orchards thronged the slopes, vines crowded in the valleys. Here the Semitic strain had received a free admixture of Greek and Phœnician; the speech of its people was fluent, idiomatic. Moreover, it was a time of great leisure, every seventh day was an idle day, every seventh year a Sabbath. The people read much in the only books they had, the Law and the Prophets, and speculated freely. Like all thinking people, they were turbulent. Recently Judas the Gaulonite headed an attempt, of amazing courage but little descretion, to break the Roman power, holding the payment of tribute little less than slavery. Two thousand of Herod's soldiers revolted. It was a time not so much of lack as of enormous social and economic disequilibrium. In short, a time very much like our own. Across the active material life of its three million population the beauty of the land struck like an inspiration. Hot harvesters lifted their foreheads to the wind that poured down from Hermon; on the lake sails glittered.

It was a fat land, but rebellious, humming with Zelots, Baptists, Essenes—a people jeoparding their life unto death. All in all an excellent field for hope to flourish in, such a hope as the man from Nazareth carried back from the Rift of Jordan, of a reconstructed social order in which imposition should wither and servitude be replaced by service. A fat land and well watered—but the taxes, the taxes! It is not prolonged underfeeding that makes revolutionists, but enforced compliance in the overfeeding of others. And here now was this new war of Herod's with its levies and impositions!

In the midst of all this Jesus went about quietly

fishing for men. He found Peter, and Andrew, his
brother, and the sons of Zebedee, owners of fishing-
smacks on Gennesaret. One thinks of him going
about, tall and personable—a figure, at least, of
which none ever complained of any lack—free striding; and a Jew, mind you, a high-nosed Jew with eyes
at once veiled and piercing, long-haired and bearded.
The hair and the beard have become so fixed in tradition that, whether or no, we must accept them.
No doubt it was one of the first pieces of personal
information that began to be circulated about him;
and they go with the temperament. One could have
found him oftenest about the water-front when the
fishing-fleet came in, clad in a long undergarment
of linen and over it a woolen mantle, brown and
white or blue, girded with leather, and always with
the turban. When he stood up in the synagogue
of a Sabbath to expound the scriptures, the linen
garment girded about the breast, the mantle would
be all white with a fringe upon it, and the long ends
of the turban floating over the hair and the mantle.
In some such guise he went about Capernaum,
sowing the Word and waiting. And at last the
thing for which he waited happened.

Herod, vexed at his failure to scatter the armies
of Aretas, and no doubt egged on by Herodias, who
must have been in a fury to have her name bruited
about at the crossroads as an adulteress, had taken

John and shut him up in prison. He shut him up
in that stark fortress which has the Dead Sea on
the west and the dead sand and black rock of
Machærus on all other sides of it; but in the face of
John's popularity, lacked hardihood to make any
other end of the matter.

There had been doubts and disaffections in Herod
the Great's time, because of his being no true Hebrew, but an Idumean. Herod characteristically
has been reported as burning up the books of geneal-
ogy in the temple, proving himself a Jew by putting
it beyond the possibility of anybody's disproving
it. But this double fear and vexation of Herod
Antipas is the true mark of Israel. John as a stirrer-
up of the people must be treated as a nuisance; as
a prophet he was to be venerated. Herod accomplished both by putting him in jail and afterward
giving his disciples access to him. So for a time the
voice of the Wilderness was stilled, but no sooner
had the news of John's imprisonment penetrated to
the rich lake region of lower Galilee than it rose
again in new accents. It was the voice of Jesus
beginning to preach openly and say, "Repent;
repent; for the Kingdom of God is at hand."

§

The rise of any great man in a community is
always an astonishment. His essential processes
are secret or obscured by ebullitions which present

themselves as offenses in the general eye. And the general eye and ear are so completely filled with their own affairs; that which finally disconcerts them and claims anew their attention is the least essential part of the message which the great have to deliver. The interest of the crowd, like the snake, darts at the thing moving.

About the end of the latter rains, when it seemed certain that the Baptist was not to be let preach again, the young carpenter, who had recently come from Nazareth, stood up in the synagogue at Capernaum and began to expound the scriptures. There had been the customary singing of psalms, the prayer beginning, "*With great love hast Thou loved us . . .*" and so down to "*Blessed be the Lord Who in love chose His people Israel.*" After that the *methurgeman* read from the Law, reading in Hebrew, in which language alone the scriptures were permitted to be written, and translating into the vernacular. There was a little light burning always in the synagogue since the captivity of Babylon, a tiny oil-fed flicker before the place where the Law was kept. It was a symbol, that little flame, of the little light that was still in Israel, feebly burning in the midst of a decadent formalism.

The light burned, the reader closed the roll of the Law, the leaders of the synagogues in the chief seats, facing the congregation, looked down their beards at their hands folded upon their knees; the women stirred faintly in the jalousied galleries; and the carpenter rose and sat in the seat of the reader. There was nothing out of the ordinary in this. Whosoever felt the Spirit of the Lord upon him was privileged to speak in the synagogue, but it was a privilege taken seriously. Perhaps nothing would have come of this particular preaching had there not been a man present afflicted with one of those forms of mental disorder which were ranked as possession by an unclean spirit. Roused by the unfamiliar figure, by something impressive and pertinent in the preacher's manner, the spirit cried out at him. Did it really cry: "I know thee who thou art, Thou Holy One of Israel!" guessing in some dim way, as the afflicted do, the man's power and destiny, or was it merely a disordered outbreak recognizing the speaker as one seen too often with Zelots and Baptists, fomenters of social discontent? "*I* know you, Jesus of Nazareth. Let us alone!" The old cry of the social unawakened. "What have we to do with thee? Thou art come to upset conditions and invite Rome to destroy us." Certainly the words would bear that interpretation. So they sounded yesterday around a soap-box on the street corner. And there were men in that congregation who could remember in the outbreak of Judas the Gaulonite the punishment Rome meted to revolutionists.   What fixed their attention on this occasion was that Jesus rebuked the interruption as the cry of uncleanness and commanded the evil spirit out of the afflicted.   They began to wonder what doctrine this could be, and to observe among themselves that he taught not as the scribes, but as one having authority.

It appears that immediately following the synagogue service Jesus went home with Simon Peter to dinner, and found Peter's wife's mother sick of a fever.   Possibly she had had a draught from a practising physician, compounded of three black spiders collected from a tomb, and an Egyptian herb or two, but it is much more likely that some neighbor had practised for her the Talmudic remedy of an iron knife tied by a braid of the sufferer's hair to a thorn-bush while reciting the first five verses of the third chapter of Exodus.   Now comes the carpenter, taking her by hand, lifting her up, and immediately the fever left her.

In order to understand how the news of such healing would spread with almost frenzied hope to the afflicted, one must pause a moment over the pitiful inefficiency of the healing art of that period.   For in that day the practice of medicine had been corrupted from the primitive knowledge of cleanliness and simples to a mass of superstition.   The cause of all sickness was a mystery, and it was believable that cures could be equally mysterious. The poor were particularly in evil case; for failing eyes there was no relief, for deformities no appliances, for anguish no twilight sleep of anesthetics, only neglect and avoidance and the unendurable pest of flies. Associated, as it had always been, with all manner of hocus-pocus, mental healing was still more reliable than the pharmacopœia of the time. Between touching the robe of a prophet and a dose of mummy powder as a specific of internal disorders, the chances of recovery were immeasurably in favor of the prophet.

As this is the first record of healing, it is probable that the exercise of it had come upon Jesus as a mere incident in the rush of spiritual certainty which had launched him upon his ministry. Filled with the power of his revelation, he had overflowed with it in the direction of the immediate human impulse and was as little prepared as any one for what followed. That evening, as soon as the sun was set and the Sabbath inhibition taken away, from every house in the neighborhood sick were brought forth and laid in the narrow street about Simon Peter's door. Here, as afterward, the man from Nazareth yielded to the appeal of human misery, but he was more than troubled by it.

No doubt he saw himself, as from this time we must think of him, as having raised the cry of universal deliverance, and hearing it drowned in the wails of immediate material anguish. As soon as it was light, without disturbing the household, he slipped away out of town; he traversed the crescent plain of Gennesaret between the stone walls and the hedges of prickly shrub, and sought the treeless foot-hill ridges. It was spring of the year, and thick dew, called the blessing of Hermon, lay on every-thing. Palms at Tiberias showed darkly against the polished lake, the olive-orchards turned the silvered under side of leaves. White fire broke out along the orchard row, anemones scarlet in the crevices, lark-spurs, blue-eyed veronica, and the hillside grass all swimming with the silken sails of poppies. Binding all the fields together ran the wild mustard, and the birds of the air lodged in its branches.

Past it all he went to the windy ridges from which one had the sea and the white slope of Her-mon, with the Jordan roaring to the deepest rift in the world far below him. Here he prayed, and here, when the day was somewhat advanced, Peter found him with the word that all men sought him. But when all was said Jesus would not go back into Capernaum.

"Let us go into the next town that I may preach there," he insisted; "for this purpose came I forth." Perhaps he still hoped to avoid the swift congre-gation of the miserable which clogged about his knees thenceforth wherever he moved; he was all bent upon his message. It was in this fashion, accompanied by Peter and those that were with him, he began to go about through the cities of Galilee, teaching in the synagogues, John being in prison, Herod in jeopardy with Aretas, Tiberius on the seat of Rome, and the destruction of Jerusalem some forty years distant.

He shall thrust out sinners from the inheritance;
he shall utterly destroy the proud spirit of the
sinners,
as a potter's vessel with a rod of iron shall he
break in pieces all their substance.

And he shall gather together a holy people whom
he shall lead in righteousness:
And he shall judge the tribe of the people that hath
been sanctified by the Lord his God.

For he shall not put his trust in the horse and
rider and bow;
nor shall he multiply unto himself gold and
silver for war;
nor by ships shall he gather confidence in the
day of battle.

Tending the flock of the Lord with faith and
righteousness;
and he shall suffer none among them to faint in
their pasture.
In holiness shall he lead them all, and there shall
be no pride among them that any should
be oppressed.

[Verses from a hymn of the Pharisees, sung during the time of Jesus and influencing the Messianic ideal. From the translation of Ryce and James.]

III

NO people can hear absolutely a new thing. The message that is delivered to them is one thing; the message heard is already half in the hearts of the hearers.

Jesus did not invent the phrase Kingdom of Heaven; what he did contrive in the course of twelve or fourteen months' teaching was to give to it entirely new meanings. As it stood in the heart of Israel it was a vision of a social order in which governorship should be of God and all temporal authority superseded by the Word. Working on this, the imagination of the time produced prodigies. More and more as the Gentile world pressed upon Jewry, it had to be accounted for; how could the Kingdom come to a people knowing not Jehovah? Opinions differed as to whether Rome should be cast into outer darkness or be permitted to feel upon her neck the heel of Jewish autonomy. It might be that the Davidic line should be restored as a mere symbol of governance, or there would be twelve thrones of the twelve princes of the House of Israel. Differences of this kind were not doctrinal; they af-

forded a pleasant variation to speculation. As the
tension of social and political unrest which ended
in the revolt and fall of Jerusalem increased, they
took on a prophet cast. It was expected that
swords should fall from heaven and come flaming in
the midst of men, the earth should yawn and all
the widening rifts be filled with dead. The apocalypse, the vision of Judgment, was a favorite form
of literature of the period.

There is a general impression that prophetic writing had ceased in Israel from the time of the old
testament to the gospels; but in fact there was a
continuous but diminishing flow of it. The Jews
had no profane history. All their writings were accounts of God in His dealings with them, either as
individuals or as a nation. Books of this kind,
bringing the story of Israel down to his own time,
were in circulation, and had been read by Jesus;
he quoted from them; from the book of Enoch he
took the title which he very early began to apply
to himself, The Son of Man.

But if no importance was attached to individual
conceptions of the Kingdom and the manner of its
inauguration, all Jewry was divided even to the
sword and the spirit about the proper preparation
for it. Theoretically Israel was a people united in
the law, one in worship; actually it was split into
sects and factions over minutiæ of fulfilment. There

was that old quarrel between the Samaritans and the Judeans concerning the mount upon which God should be worshiped, which had resulted, in the time of Cyrenius, in the Samaritans being disbarred from the temple. There were at least two ascetic orders, the Nazarites and Essenes—of whom the first were as old as the time of the prophets—men dedicate to God from birth and sometimes before it, drinking no wine, celibate, cutting neither the hair nor the beard. They walked apart and sought out God in their own hearts.

The Essenes lived in communities, repudiated marriage for themselves, but adopted children, prayed before and after meals, wore white, and had a sense of caste which made the touch of lower orders a defilement. They made no sacrifice except of their desires, devoted themselves to good works and practised healing. They had community houses in all the large cities. It is not unlikely that as a lad the carpenter's son had gone to school to them, a kind of friar's school where one learned to read the scriptures and be truthful, chaste, and obedient.

Though they served to color the religious thought of the time, in numbers both Nazarites and Essenes were inconsiderable. The great body of the Jews were either Pharisees or Sadducees. These last were mainly of aristocratic and priestly families.

They held a practical monopoly of the Sanhedrin and the priestly offices, repudiating life after death, disbelieving God as far as anybody of that time dared disbelieve Him. Opportunists, bent upon maintaining their own rights and privileges, they were sensitive to popular disorder lest it give the Romans an excuse for removing them.

Against these were the Pharisees, the aristocracy of moral assumption. So successful had they been in putting over on the masses the conviction of their superior virtue that as patterns they had largely superseded the priesthood; in company with the Scribes, those scholarly and pedantic searchers of the scriptures, they set, as it were, the fashions in moral behavior. Their fields of action were chiefly the Rabbinical schools, where they taught that there is an immortal vigor in man which can be nourished to rewards or punishments in the life beyond this. Over-nice in their liturgical observances, they were nevertheless the conservers of what was left of the ancient Jewish integrity.

In addition to these, in Galilee there were two fire-new vessels of social discontent: the following of the Baptist, among whom we reckon the man from Nazareth, and the adherents of Judas, called the Zelot, a considerable band who went mad with the abuse of authority under Gessius Florius, the procurator, who were reported not to value death nor any kind of dying so long as they might call no man lord. They "had an inviolable attachment to liberty," and for the rest they agreed with the moral teachings of the Pharisees.

Over all was the hand of Rome, penetrating even into the dreams of men, so that they could not so much as imagine Heaven except in the terms of kingdoms and authority.

Into all this welter of formalism and self-seeking, formalism and piety, into attempted Hellenic culture and hole-in-the-corner asceticism the man from Nazareth poured out his message, to meet and contend with it, and be set back in its course like a stream pouring into the sea, finally to mix with it so that never any more could its meaning be traced clear until men should cease seeking at the meeting of the waters in the muddled Word, but turn back to the immortal source of the Spirit.

It is a mistake, however, to think of Jesus at the outset of his career as opposed to all this; he was an inextricable part of it. Himself an avowed Baptist, there is some reason to believe that he held himself *Nazar*, vowed, set apart for God; he borrowed freely from the practices of the Essenes. It is probable that the family at Nazareth was pharisaical in the best sense, leaning a little to the too scrupulous fulfilment of the law rather than to a neglect of it. His brother James, at least, turned out a great pietist,

and, though he suffered a martyr's death, is described
as wearing callouses on his knees praying in the
temple for the spread of Christianity.

At least one of the disciples was a Zelot, and probably all of them Baptists.   One guesses that a certain aloofness discernible in the beginning of his
ministry was actuated by the desire of Jesus to free
himself from all these tangled and entangling lines
of influence.

None of these, however, gave him so personal a
difficulty as the effort to prevent his teaching from
being swamped in the immediate human demand
for material relief.   After the opening of his ministry
in Capernaum he made a tour of the neighboring
cities, preaching in the synagogues and suffering
similar interruptions.

A leper, to whom knowledge of the new prophet's
healing power had come, followed him across the
fields, protesting, "If thou wilt thou canst make me
clean."   It was not an extravagant confidence.
The liturgical detail to be observed by a leper who
has been cleansed is too complete not to warrant
the conclusion that mental healing of leprosy was
possible, even frequent, in Palestine. Although
Jesus avoided healing, it is not of record that, once
the afflicted succeeded in gaining his attention, he
ever refused relief.   On this occasion the faith of the
leper and the compassion of the prophet were equal;

but the caution to tell no man broke down before the natural flow of gratitude.

As the healed leper returned from showing himself to the priest, and performing those things for his own relief and the protection of the community as prescribed by Moses, the news burst from him. It spread through all the countryside and forthwith the preacher was engulfed again in the rising tide of human anguish. It drove him out from the cities to the hill places where only the strong could come to him. Shepherds heard him as they went with their flocks white from the spring shearing to feed on the plains of Esdraelon, wood-cutters going up toward Hermon, and a continual trickle from the towns, for, says the recorder, "all men were in expectation," straining toward the last struggle for Jewish autonomy. He visited Nazareth, preaching the acceptable year of the Lord, and discovered that a prophet is not without honor save in his own country, for, said the Nazarenes, "Is not this the carpenter?" Luke says they hustled him, but I find this incompatible with his ironic tolerance. The pinch of bitterness was yet to come.

It was after some weeks of this, when he returned to Capernaum, that there occurred the first of those encounters with established order which led on to his destruction and the final elevation of his message above the accidents of flesh. The house to which he had come, not his own, but possibly Peter's, was so thronged with those who wished to hear and so besieged from the narrow street without, that it was impossible for late comers to have access to him. But there was a man sick of the palsy whose desire for healing was equaled by his faith in the man from Nazareth to accomplish it. If they could only get at him! By this times Jesus' avoidance of publicity must have become a matter of general knowledge, for the sick man's friends took no chance of meeting the prophet on the public highway. They ascended by way of one of the flat, shoulder-to-shoulder houses, and from the roof let down the bed through the open, middle court which is the distinctive feature of Oriental dwellings.

Now was the wished-for moment when the prophet, moved by their faith and taking compassion on the sick of the palsy, should say, "Take up thy bed and walk," but, lying there with all eyes upon him, the expectant sufferer heard a thing even more amazing. Said Jesus, "Thy sins be forgiven thee."

It is possible that this was more germane to the case than appears from the meager account of it; whether or no this palsy was one of those nervous collapses which are the effect of excess, and had its seat deeper in the man's soul than in his quaking body, cannot now be more than suggested. Whether the remission of sin was addressed to the sufferer

or beyond him to the waiting audience, it did strike
across and reached the Scribes that, with how much
of honest inquiry who can guess, had turned out to
hear the new prophet.   A Scribe was in some sort
a councilor of the law when one of the parties to
the case was God Almighty.   He was versed in all
minutiæ of the scriptures and in nice interpretations.
It was from the Scribes that the Pharisees derived
authority for all that punctilious observance by
the exercise of which they assumed the virtues that
no longer sprang spontaneously from their barren
breasts.   By a process which may be observed going
on in our own day among legal interpreters, the
work of the Scribes had narrowed to the business of
ascertaining just how far a man may push the
letter of the law in his favor without incurring any
of its penalties.   Now as they heard this so quietly
uttered and so extraordinary statement, there ran
a whisper from one to another: "Who can forgive
sins but God— Oh, blasphemy!" and there was a
great wagging of turbans.

"Think you," said the man from Nazareth, "it is
easier to say thy sins be forgiven thee, or to say, arise,
take up thy bed and walk?"

And getting no answer from them, he continued,
"That you may know that the son of man *has*
power on earth to forgive sins, I say unto thee, arise,
take up thy bed and go thy way into thine house."

As the sick man arose and went forth before them all, carrying his bed, there went forth with him the most revolutionary doctrine which had yet been pronounced among men. *The son of man has power on earth to forgive sins.* For observe that up to this time Jesus had not spoken of himself as the Appointed One, nor assumed for himself any character but that of preacher of an urgent word. There is no evidence that in the title, Son of Man, by which he referred to himself, he meant to express anything but the merging of his personality in his social function; to speak not as Jesus of Nazareth, but as heir of all the ages, a fraction of that close-woven human fabric of which he at all times warmly felt himself a part. Later in his career he was to come back to this point and reiterate what was here so lightly indicated, the *community* of power, equally accessible to himself and his disciples—"Greater things than these shall ye do"—a power which even during his lifetime, under his instruction, they began to exercise. "Man," he said, "*hath* power...."

It was no new thing for one man, by some process not yet fully understood, to reach across to another and so stir up the centers of his being as to set back the whole course of nature and effect a profound reorganization of the physical forces. That such a thing can be done is a common and ancient piece of human knowledge. But from times older than

Israel it has been recognized that deep personal disaster can be traced to violations of laws which lie beyond the minor infringements of bodily illness and are amenable only to the forgiveness of offended deity. There is always the chance of evading the consequences of such a violation by persuading the gods, or by setting them one against another, but a small chance and exceedingly uncertain. Pagan and Hebrew alike brooded under a sense of inescapable destiny.

The doctrine that plain man could by plain man his brother be released from spiritual bondage fell upon soil so unprepared that twenty centuries of harrowing have produced but a few thin sprouts from it. By what power resident in man, by what paths it is attained, was to be developed as a later part of his teaching. The disciples of Jesus perceived it only as a cloud on the eastern horizon. There was the thing before them in its concrete example of the man with the palsy, but the principle in its utter simplicity escaped them as the perfect pearl eludes the hand by its roundness.

It is impossible, however, to twist out of this incident any other meaning than that such release should pass from man to man. At that time Jesus gave no evidence of thinking of himself as other than his companions except in the authority and singleness of his calling; all that he professed was the complete interpenetration of what we have agreed to call matter and spirit. It was a simpler and more direct form of what society begins to practise fumblingly, like a novice with a new instrument,—the freeing of man by man: the criminal from the compulsion of his criminal nature, the obsessed from his evil obsession, the incompetent from his incompetency, and, Heaven save the mark! the poor from his poverty. About the much more advanced movement to free man from the violation of his physical nature by means of the spirit that is in him, I say nothing. It is among us in a form to admit of personal investigation on every side. We are tolerant of it as in their day were the Scribes and the Pharisees, and tolerant for the same reason; we know that it has been done, but we are unfamiliar with and suspicious of the instrument. It is reported by one John Mark, who is described as having written down all that he could remember of what Peter told him of this occasion, that the launching of this revolutionary truth was accompanied with nothing more than a general amazed comment on the part of the Capernaumites that never in their lives had they seen things done in this fashion.

§

By this time, which could not have been more than six months after his baptism, Jesus appears to have broadened the scope of preparation for the

kingdom without having lost his sense of its immanence. On the way to his own house after the
incident of the man sick of the palsy, he passed the
office of the local tax-collector; one of those minor
officials to whom the Roman imposition was farmed
out after a fashion which rendered Rome so ob-
noxious to conquered nations. It was an office
hated not only for what it was, but for what it stood
for in the community; the constant menace of life
and liberty in an age when death, mutilation, and
the selling of whole families into slavery were ad-
judged not too severe punishments for delinquents.
This Matthew, who from the description of him as
"sitting at the receipt of customs" may have been
a collector of imposts between Galilee and Perea
which lay along the eastern shore of the lake, had
not yet been corrupted by his office, for the next
we hear of him he is sitting at supper with Jesus
and others of his following.

It was the custom in Oriental countries, in the
absence of universities and public forums, for learned
men to gather about them groups of disciples, sitting for disquisition on the housetops or at meat
in the still, cool upper chambers. This was the
practice of rabbis in Israel, only in Israel there was
nothing recognized as learning which did not concern itself with God and human conduct. Gather-
ings of this sort at the house of Jesus in Capernaum

must have been of another sort than the slow, ordered discussions of Hillel and Shamai at Jerusalem, meetings full of hope and high-keyed expectation, looking toward the kingdom.

Simon the Zelot would be there, the impetuous
Peter, and the two sons of Zebedee, nicknamed the
Sons of Thunder, those impatient souls who would
have called down fire from heaven on the villages
which would not receive the prophet on his journey
up to Jerusalem. There were also in that company
Matthew the publican, whose business so discredited
him with society that his evidence would not be
taken in court, and other doubtful characters; sitting
in the head of the board, the carpenter, witty, genial,
sanguine, seeing Heaven in their midst and the great
day so close at hand that they would scarcely have
gone through the cities of Israel before it should be
upon them. Whatever it was that went on in the
house of Jesus, it was exciting enough or important
enough for all Capernaum to be set gossiping
over it.

"How is it," carped the Scribes and Pharisees,
"that this man sits eating and drinking with low
fellows, publicans and sinners?" One suspects that
the Pharisees had rather adopted the new preacher
in the beginning—for a prophet might arise—and
it was more than their sense of prophetic propriety
which was slighted. But Jesus when he heard of it

sent them word that he had come not to call the righteous, but sinners. Said he, "They that are whole need not a physician; but they that are sick," one of those flashes of gentle irony so characteristic of him, for if there was any class in Israel that was sick unto death with formalism it was the Scribes and Pharisees. But another thing troubled them, and in this there was no doubt a measure of honest questioning. "John fasted," they said, "and the Pharisees fast, but why not thy disciples?"

There must be a special dispensation somewhere for those poor souls who would like to know the truth, if only they could recognize it in an unfamiliar garment. Said Jesus, "Can the children of the bridechamber fast, while the bridegroom is with them? . . ." Also he said that no man seweth a piece of new cloth on an old garment, lest the new piece tear away that to which it is sewed and the rent is made worse, and no man putteth new wine in old bottles, lest the bottles burst and the wine is spilled and the bottles marred. It was in this fashion that he placed the definite mark of modernism between himself and the Baptist. Whether or not he recognized the fullness of his message and its revolutionary character, he at least understood that it was a mistake to follow John in attempting to pour it into the old Levitical mold. Jesus came preaching the Kingdom but with new meanings and new manners. His vision on that point was perfectly clear, but the circumstance was too much for him. With his new cloth the ancient fabric of Hebraism was torn asunder, he poured his new wine into as many new bottles as could be found, and still the bottles burst.

Extra - canonical sayings of Jesus from early Christian writings, probably genuine, or founded on true sayings.

In whatsoever things I discover you, in these will I also judge you.—Justin Martyr.

Ask the great things and the small shall be added unto you; ask the heavenly and the earthly shall be added unto you.—Clement of Alexander.

On account of them that are infirm I was infirm, and on account of them that hunger did I hunger, and on account of them that thirst did I thirst.—Origen.

On the same day he beheld one working on the Sabbath and said unto him, O man, if thou knowest what thou art doing, blessed art thou; but if thou knowest not, thou art accursed and a transgressor of the law.—Codex Bezae.

IV

WE shall have to go back to this remedial use of the Spirit as between man and man, called forgiveness of sins, but we must have more to go upon. From the time that Jesus came under the influence of John to his declaration of a superior freedom of personal conduct, the sequence of events is clear, but the preaching is lost to us. That so little is recalled as being definitely placed in this period would imply that his audiences were small and his converts few in number. But at Capernaum he was again the object of public attention. He met here with that most coveted distinction of the revolutionist, opposition from the established order.

Both opposition and interest centered about these two points: his neglect of Levitical formalities and his work as a healer. It was not that he failed to appreciate the value of ceremonial—there is a custom of blessing bread before breaking it which is mentioned often enough to point the inference that Jesus observed it, and we find him paying the temple tax and keeping the great festivals of Israel with due observance—but he went through the fabric

61

of pharisaical formality like a lion of Judah through a net set to catch fieldfares. It was only when he felt it enclosing the lesser personalities of his disciples that he stooped to justification. That was how we find him about the first of June of the year that began his ministry, walking with his disciples of a Sabbath morning, probably between village and village, that he might preach at the morning and evening services, and passing on their way the fields of standing corn now whitening for the harvest. Perhaps the time was all too short for the customary midday meal, or the zeal of the preacher sometimes outran the nature of the apostles, for they, being ahungered, broke off and threshed out between thumb and palm the wheaten ears and ate them.

Now a man might not be condemned under the law for failing to fast, but threshing grain on the Sabbath . . . here at last they had him! Here again Jesus defined for his accusers those principles of spiritual efficiency which determined all his conduct. "The Sabbath," said he, "was made for man, not man for the Sabbath." He also answered them a little more in their own key with a scriptural reference to what David did in the matter of the shewbread in the temple. It is doubtful, however, if the exposition cleared the subject levitically any more than it confused humanly with this easy comparison of kings and carpenters.

Silenced they were, but not answered, for we read that a little later, possibly on the same Sabbath or the next one, he was teaching in the synagogue, and a man with a withered hand, posted there for that purpose, asked of him a healing. Fully aware of an intention to trap him into Sabbath-breaking, for which in any notable degree he might be brought before the authorities, Jesus turned them face to face again with the spirit of that law by the letter of which they hoped to snare him. "What man of you that have a sheep fall into a pit on the Sabbath will he not lay hold to lift it out? . . . and is not man more than a sheep?" There was more from the same source, but the Pharisees looked down their noses, unable to refute the argument and unwilling to admit it. It is the first time of record that Jesus showed himself indignant with his audience; reaching out his hand to the stricken man, he lifted him from the pit of his own affliction.

We who are the inheritors of generations of prejudice against the class who opposed Jesus, need to remind ourselves that there is somewhat to be said in extenuation. The Pharisees were a people doing the best they knew to fulfil what they recognized as the supreme obligation—the will of Jehovah. Much that they did was done in anticipation of that closer union of God and Israel which was to be affected in the person of the Messiah. They served

God as much as they were able and expected God to honor the alliance. Now here was this man of the common people, putting all their strained conformities to shame, and yet distinguished by God with the insigna of a true prophet. Not that they cared what the carpenter could do, but if this man were truly a prophet or, as began to be whispered, the Messiah, then had God passed them over. How the slight must have rankled! Would they believe it of God after all their meticulous service? Not they! Some other explanation must be found of the extraordinary phenomenon, and one was not long in forthcoming.

Shortly after the healing of the withered hand on the Sabbath, and possibly to escape the controversy stirred up by it, Jesus set sail upon Gennesaret for the opposite leopard-colored shore of Gadara. Here the hills broke off abruptly, full of caves, with little ledges of limestone running into the lake and little spits of sand breaking the shore. Swineherds fed their despised charges hereabouts; the caves were inhabited by lepers and the insane. What occurred there has come to us so mixed with popular superstition of the time that it is impossible to thresh out from it the modicum of fact, and perhaps not important. It was what people thought had happened that affected their attitude toward the teacher. It seems, however, that the man from

Nazareth was immediately recognized and appealed to by one of the most unfortunate of that unfriended class, the demoniacs. It was so that all manner of mental and nervous derangements were described, as possession by evil spirits, a belief that Jesus seems to have shared. One such very pitiful case was healed here on the Gadarean shore under circumstances that excited the utmost superstitious awe of him, so much so that deputations came out from the cities round about and entreated him to depart out of their coasts.

It was this incident and some others like it which gave rise to the charge which was presently brought against him, that he cast out demons by the help of the very Powers of Darkness. The logic of Jesus that a devil casting out devils would be a house divided against itself, served not only to silence opposition for the moment, but to augment the popular favor. All Galilee was aflame. Samaria heard of him. He seems almost to have been constrained to accepting the significance of his healing at the common estimate, without, however, losing his remarkable poise and sanity.

The daughter of a centurion fell sick—at Capernaum, no doubt, where a garrison was stationed—and the Roman, backed by the good word of his Hebrew neighbors, dared appeal to Jesus. By the time, however, that the prophet had reached the house the child's condition was such that the rumor of her death touched with hysteria the ill-balanced Oriental household. To an impostor such an opportunity would have been irresistible. Dead certainly; and now behold a miracle! But the man from Nazareth, quietly reassuring, passed through the crowds of excited domestics to the inner chamber. "She is not dead," said he, "but sleeping." Having taken her by the hand and roused her, he bade them in a perfectly common-sense manner give her something to eat and say no more about it. Out of this, which could not be kept entirely private, the common tongue multiplied wonders. The tide of enthusiasm rose and rolled over all parts of Judea, even as far as Idumea. It reached John in his lonely prison; it rose almost to his own head.

Crowds poured into Capernaum from the surrounding country, they thronged him in the street if they might so much as touch his garment. Wherever he moved the sick were laid out along his path, happy even to feel his shadow in passing. The tide of popular appreciation rose higher; it overflowed the narrow streets of the lake town and reached even to the hills of Nazareth. His people heard of his doings and came down to take him home with them. Said they, "He is beside himself." In nothing so much have they confirmed the family status; it was so exactly like what would be expected of the leading family in a small town who had borne on their branches the greatest radical of their time. It is the last word as to their entire respectability. But Jesus made himself inaccessible in the midst of his disciples, and when word was brought to him that his brethren were without, seeking for him, he answered them, saying, "Who is my mother or my brethren?" And looking round on those which sat about him, he said: "Behold my mother and my brethren! For whosoever shall do the will of God the same is my brother and my sister and my mother."

It must have been about this time that John called two of his disciples and sent to him, saying, "Art thou he that should come, or look we for another?"

Now he that should come was the long-prophesied Messiah, the Anointed One, who was to restore the kingdom to Israel, concerning whose advent John had borne witness. It was a natural and inevitable question. It had been asked of John, who had himself been under no illusion as to the nature of his own calling. It was probably already being asked under the breath by believers of Jesus. From the answer he returned to the Baptist's inquiry, it seems likely that Jesus might have asked it in all humility of himself. For his answer when it came, was neither an affirmation nor a denial: "Go your way," he said,

"tell John what things ye have seen and heard,
how the blind see, the lame walk, the lepers are
cleansed, the deaf hear, and to the poor the gospel
is preached!"

All this is immensely interesting in view of what
Jesus is known elsewhere to have said and indicated
as to the relative place of his power to heal in his
work as a teacher. From the beginning he seems
to have regarded it as incident to his career rather
than an integral part of it. He never ascribed it to
any other power than the uninterrupted working of
the Father in him. He never thought of it as a gift
peculiar to himself, but attainable by any man
who let himself be utterly shone through by the
spirit that was in Jesus. For its complete operation
he recognized the necessity of some sort of conjunc-
tion between the healer and the patient. Ordinarily
this was accomplished by establishing belief between
them—the desire to be healed accompanied by the
firm conviction on both sides that healing was possible. "Believest thou?" and, "According to thy
faith be it unto thee," were his most frequent for-
mulas; but he did not neglect to assist the faith of
the applicant by material means when necessary.
It is related of the first leper that applied to him,
that Jesus touched him. To touch a leper was not
only a Levitical defilement, but a practical menace.
It was because of this liability to contagion that

they were required to go about crying, "Unclean, unclean!" in an isolation more terrible than death.

Nothing then could have been better calculated to raise the faith of the unfortunate than that fearless human contact. To Jesus the leper *was* clean; and almost immediately he became so to himself.

Later, when his work as a healer appears to have been overborne by his message and the unresponsiveness of the community, he used symbolic acts, such as touchings, anointings of the eyes, to create that rapport between him and his patient which was so important to success. Also it is recorded that in more than one town he did no mighty work because of their unbelief.

Although he once spoke in reference to a stubborn case of possession, of aid to be derived from prayer and fasting—he had just come on that occasion from a long session of spiritual communion— he seems never to have related the work of healing to any sort of goodness, any preferred frame of moral behavior. For we read that at the cleansing of the temple, in his most human outburst of indignation, in that same hour they brought to him lame and blind, and he healed them.

It is also indisputable that Jesus taught that healing could be sought by one for another; the faith of the parent for the child, of the master for

the servant, acted as the solvent of disorder, or, if
you prefer it, as the conductor of the divine inunda-
tion.   Two or three instances of this sort shall be
noted in their proper order; we have here to do with
Jesus' own opinion as to what his healing powers
witnessed. He offered them to John as the only
available evidence, and in the same series, that the
poor had the gospel preached to them. Is it too
much to conclude that in offering the facts of his
ministry rather than its message, his teaching was
as yet differentiated from John's only by being an
extension of it?   In a beautiful tribute to the Baptist
which is reported to us by Luke, he places John at the
forefront of the tribe of prophets. "Among those
born of women . . . not a greater. . . ."   If it is the case
that John was the first to teach that the Kingdom
of God is affected by relations between man and
man, rather than between man and deity, the judgment of time would seem to agree with him. "But
he that is least in the kingdom of God is greater
than he." If by this Jesus meant that the man who
realizes in his daily life that perfect balance between
man and his neighbor which is the essence of Christianity, is greater than he who merely announces it,
here too history is in accord. John appears to us
as a man who rather escaped such realization by
his life in the Wilderness; but his disciple Jesus
accomplished it.

This is almost the last we shall hear of the Baptist, for it was not far from the time when he should lose his life under Herod, the King himself being reluctant, but trapped into beheading him by that Herodias whom John's preaching had so offended. It was fitting that this tribute should come from his most distinguished convert, and one reads with satisfaction that it was received with enthusiasm by the disciples of Jesus, many of whom had been baptized with John's baptism. And for the Pharisees and lawyers who rejected the counsel of God against themselves, there was one of those brilliant thrusts which, while it rendered his critics silent, always the more deeply enraged them. Said the Master:

Whereunto shall I liken the men of this generation,
And to what are they like?

They are like unto children sitting in the market place
Calling to one another and saying,
We have piped unto you and ye have not danced;
We have mourned unto you and ye have not wept,

For John the Baptist came
Neither eating bread nor drinking wine,
And ye say, He hath a devil;

The Son of man is come eating and drinking,
And ye say, Behold a gluttonous man, a wine-
      bibber,
A friend of Publicans and sinners.

But Wisdom is justified of all her children!

§

Among other things accomplished during the
second stay in Capernaum was the raising of the
number of his personal following to twelve in remembrance of the twelve houses of Israel. Their organization was of the simplest; they had a common
purse and were the recipients of his most intimate
teaching. In nothing so much has Jesus shown his
humanness to be of the same stripe as that of all
great geniuses as in this selection; for of the twelve,
one betrayed him and only two or three after his
death showed any especial aptitude for the dissemina-
tion of his doctrine.

But seeing all Israel as sheep lacking a shepherd,
he seized upon what seemed the likeliest material,
and within a month or two began to send them
forth to the cities of Galilee.

About the end of the barley harvest, if we accept
the chronology which the color of his speech allows,
they drew out of the plain of Gennesaret to one of
those hollow cone-shaped hills of upper Galilee,
having on its outer rim twin towering peaks like

the frontlet of a bull, called the Horns of Hattin.
It is reached by a foot-path up through the Valley
of Doves, between thickets of oak and thorn and
oleander. Here the twelve came for their parting
instruction, but not unmarked by that crowd of
miserables who seem to have hung always about his
path, ready to pounce upon the first faint hope of
healing. Where the blind and the halt and the sick
borne in litters were seen moving in any given direction, there the crowd came hurrying. They
must have been at it all the warm, star-lighted dusk,
threading the dim trails, for when Jesus, after a
night spent in prayer apart on one of the peaks,
came down into the amphitheater, he found it filled
with the multitude. Accounts differ as to what he
said to them, but all agree that the occasion was
notable and that he met it with a more than ordinary
accession of preaching power. They agree, too, in
presenting the sermon delivered between the Horns
of Hattin as a practical direction for the conduct of
life rather than a doctrinal disquisition. Something
of the sort the setting out of the disciples called for:
and in the manner of coming together of the crowd
there was evinced a demand for instruction more explicit than the mere announcement of the kingdom.
Time and place had combined to make it the sin-
cerest and best-selected audience that had yet collected about the prophet.

Whether the things recorded as the sermon on the mount were first said there, or elsewhere, or whether, as seems likely, they were things said and repeated on various occasions, is unimportant. Some of them were undoubtedly framed to meet the exigencies of the twelve on their preaching tours; but all in all the discourse stands as the most consistent program of Christian character that had yet been offered.

It seems to have begun with a rush to meet the unvoiced demand that was made upon the teacher by their simply being there at such pains and in such numbers, anxious-hearted; by the marks upon them of the conditions under which life was lived in Palestine, the personal tyrannies, the grinding impositions.

"Blessed are ye, O ye poor," he cried, "for yours is the kingdom of heaven. Blessed are ye that do hunger and thirst, for ye shall be filled. . . ." And one whose need was bread heard it as a promise of material relief, and whoso thirsted for the things of the spirit heard it as pertaining to the Spirit. To others who lacked everything it came as the promise of the kingdom which was to come only Heaven knew how, but very shortly, a proletariat Heaven in which the poor were to be rich and the rich poor, and everything quite and completely different. Taken with other things that he said then and upon later occasions, I can make nothing more or less of it than the involuntary expression of his bright belief in the abundance of God lying open *in all things* to whoever would reach out and seize them. For he said again: "Take no thought what ye shall eat, nor yet for your body what ye shall put on . . . for if God so clothe the grass of the field. . . . O ye of little faith!" And again: "For your Heavenly Father knoweth you have need of these things. Seek ye therefore the kingdom of God and all these things shall be added unto you."

All his early teaching was vibrant with this joyous confidence of the Spirit to compel the flow of material things—health, food, and raiment. He poured it out here, flashing his discourse now upon the twelve and now to the waiting multitude, and again sweeping them all into the compass of the hand as children of the Father. "Ye are the light of the world," he said. "Let your light so shine among men. . . ."

For he was not come to destroy the law, but to fulfil it in terms of the thoughts and affections of men. They were not to think that the law against murder was to be kept by the mere avoidance of killing, but by the denial of hate and anger and all forms of enmity; it was not alone in incontinence of the flesh that unchastity consisted, but in the lusts of the eye and the imaginations of the heart. This was sterner doctrine to Israel than to us after a score of centuries, but the probe went even deeper. It struck at the very root of Hebrew morality, that austere and measured system of reprisal upon which their civil code was founded, an eye for an eye and a tooth for a tooth. *Vengeance is mine saith the Lord*; *I will repay;* and as they expected God to deal with them so dealt they with their fellows. "But I say unto you," ran the new teaching, "love your enemies, do good to them that hate you and pray for them that despitefully use you."

In the multiplicity of points at which it touched their daily life, this was even a more revolutionary doctrine than that of the forgiveness of sins. But perhaps just because of its nearness they understood it better. This can be gathered from the readiness with which, after his death had sealed it to them, the early Christians practised the new teaching; they were not as we are, put at fault by the free imagery in which it was stated.

"Whosoever will smite thee on thy right cheek turn to him thy left also," said Jesus, "and whosoever shall compel thee to go a mile with him, go twain." But in the different accounts of it the context of this saying is changed. One suspects some crossing here of general principles and the special direction intended for the disciples who were about to set out on an errand in which it was important that no antagonism should be aroused. Jesus himself always went the second mile with his adversaries, and at the end of it defeated them. The whole of that passage beginning "resist not evil," reads more like the best example of that spiritual astuteness that distinguished him than a declaration of religious principle. Wise as serpents and harmless as doves, they were to find in non-resistance the subtlest, completest form of victory. At least the passage was never interpreted by the men who heard it, as a doctrine of inaction. Both Jesus and his disciples were sharp in attack on existing evils, fearless in denunciation, not devoid of just wrath, and active in proselyting.

So much of the sermon as we have glanced at was constructive. The rest of it was mainly taken up with precept and illustration touching the peculiar weaknesses of the time, hypocrisy and formalism. Alms were to be given in secret, not to be seen of men; so also of prayer, which he enjoined on them. In the closet with shut door they were to seek the Father, and, seeking, they should find; knocking, it should be opened unto them. "For if ye, being evil, know how to give good gifts to your children, how much more shall your Father which is in Heaven give good things to them that ask him."

These were the sayings of Jesus set down by

Matthew and John Mark in answer to the first
eager cry of converts, "What shall I *do* to be saved?"
For there was never any doubt on the part of those
who listened to Jesus and his disciples that partici-
pation in the kingdom was dependent upon a
changed conduct, "Except your righteousness ex-
ceed the righteousness of the Scribes and Pharisees . . ." and again, "Not every one that heareth, but
he that *doeth* the will of my Father." That is why,
perhaps, we have in the gospels so much of specific
direction and less than we would gladly hear of the
spiritual illumination from which it proceeds. For
it is impossible not to realize how little resemblance
there is between the God of love whom Jesus came
preaching and the Jehovah of the Hebrew scriptures,
jealous, capricious, avenging, worshiped with bloody
rites at Jerusalem, with scapegoat and sin-offering
and burnt-offering of bullocks and of rams. It was
not in either of the great Jewish sects that he found
the doctrine of man in God and God in man, as implied in the terms of kinship used by Jesus. Yet
in none of the gospels is it set down as a new doctrine,
nor was the preacher ever called to account for it.
Though there is some reason to believe that he regarded it as an important part of his mission to
make known the true nature of God, Jesus himself
never explained when or by what means he had
come by the revelation. It was one of those truths

which lie at the bottom of the deep wells of human understanding, so native to its element, so intrinsic that, once realized, it is not thought of as requiring explication. With something of the same simplicity with which it was offered, the fatherliness of God was accepted. But your true Oriental is always a mystic. It was easier for him to realize that "no man knoweth the Father save only the son"—that is to say, that only by the God-in-man is the God-beyond-man apprehended—than it was to understand how the kingdom of God could be set up in Israel without the physical overthrow of the Roman Empire. The sermon on the mount instructed those who heard it in the sort of behavior which at the same time fitted for the approaching kingdom of heaven and provided a way of escape from destruction, but in respect to the scope and manner of that kingdom when it should come, it left them exactly where it found them.

Give not that which is holy unto dogs
  Neither cast your pearls before swine,
Lest haply the swine trample them under foot
  And the dogs turn and rend you.
                    —Matt. vii, 6.

By their fruits ye shall know them.
  Do men gather grapes of thorns?
  Or figs of thistles?
  Even so every good tree bringeth forth good fruit
  But the corrupt tree bringeth forth evil fruit:
  A good tree can not bring forth evil fruit,
  Neither can a corrupt tree bring forth good fruit.
  Every tree that bringeth not forth good fruit
  Is hewn down and cast into the fire.
Therefore by their fruits ye shall know them.
                    —vii, 16-20.

No servant can serve two masters:
  For either he will hate the one
    And love the other;
    Or else he will hold to one
  And despise the other.

He can not serve God and Mammon.
                    —Luke xvi, 13.

[Original form of sayings of Jesus. Arranged by Richard
G. Moulton.]

V

OF what happened to the twelve on their tour, who heard and who reviled them, there is not so much as a tradition. They went forth to do as they saw Jesus doing—to teach, to heal, and to cast out devils; at no point was the business of the disciple distinguished from that of the master. It was evident from the instruction they received that they were not to go far nor to remain long; they came again and told all that they had done.

Of what happened to Jesus in the interim there is even less, unless we place in this period some incidents not otherwise located except by the logic of circumstance. Of these the most significant was the supper at the house of a Pharisee. It seems more probable that after his return from the mountain, rid of his immediate following, men of no very great refinement of manner if the truth must be told, certain of the Pharisees who had been attracted by his doctrine but repelled by his want of conformity, would again attempt to put themselves in sympathy with the prophet.

One did so attempt by inviting him to his house

for a meal; and while it was in progress, possibly in the open court, for it was now full summer, the guests reclining in the Roman manner—for so it was the custom of the Jews at their feasts to assume the postures of free men—there came a woman into the room and stood behind the Master. She stood there weeping in the dusk; her tears fell upon his feet, and she wiped them with her hair.   They could see her in the flare of the tall lamps, wiping his feet and kissing them, and presently the air of the place began to be filled with perfume, delicate and costly. Then the Pharisee said in his heart, for he knew her, "If this man were a prophet"—for he was by no means sure—"he would know what manner of woman this is, for she is a sinner," but though it was his own house, he dared not be the first to speak of it.

He watched for some movement of withdrawal on the part of his guest, from the defiling presence, but instead he found himself addressed.

"Simon, I have somewhat to say to thee."

"Say on, Master."

Said Jesus: "There was a certain creditor had two debtors, the one of whom owed five hundred pence, the other fifty, and when they had nothing to pay, he frankly forgave them both. Tell me therefore, which of them will love him most."

"I suppose he to whom he forgave most."   Simon

was ready enough with the answer, but he saw not where the question tended.

At the beginning he had omitted those attentions which were due an honored guest, fearing, perhaps, to commit himself too much. The man *might* be a prophet, in which case it were well to have entertained him, but still— And now his guest was pointing out to him that it was the woman who had supplied the missing hospitality, the ceremonial washing, the kiss of welcome, the anointing.

"Wherefore," said the Master, "her sins are forgiven, for she hath loved much; but he to whom little is forgiven, the same loveth little." And to the woman he said: "Go in peace; thy sins be forgiven thee." This was the way he took to turn even the slights of his adversaries to advantage in the spread of his doctrine. It was also one of the things that was remembered against him.

How else he spent the time of his disciples' absence cannot be so much as guessed, unless he spent a part of it in his mother's house at Nazareth. The last we hear of his family was on the occasion of their visit to him at Capernaum, when, if he received them at all, it was not until after they had been made to feel that their claim upon him was less than that of more ardent believers. And the next we hear is that Mary his mother, and possibly a brother, are in the group that followed him up to Jerusalem.

James was martyred for his sake, and the grandsons of Jude confessed him as Christ before the Emperor Domitian.

There must have intervened between these, some occasion on which his family had leisure to hear and be converted by him, and this is the only unaccounted-for interval of his ministry.

It would probably have been during this period of retirement that the news reached him of how the daughter of Herodias had danced the head of John the Baptist off his shoulders and on to a silver charger, otherwise there would have been some public question raised by it. And if he were not where I suppose him, then he was more than likely where we read that he was often to be found, apart in the hills and desert places at prayer.

It is not because the soul of man is less importunate, but only because it is immensely more fluent than the physical habit, that his religious practices take their cast from his daily living. Ordinarily the spirit accommodates itself to trifles of custom and expedient as a stream to the pebbles in its bed, flowing over and around them; it is only in freshets that they are carried utterly away. The essential teachings of the man Joshua Ben Joseph cut a wide, free channel for the spiritual aspirations of the time, but his private religious observances were largely shaped by contemporaneous Hebrew usage.

The pagan carried his gods with him. Every place in which he elected to set up his altars became sacred, fit for worship or expiation; but to the Jew there was but one holy place, even the mount of Jerusalem. Only between the horns of the great altar could sacrifice be acceptably made. But ever since the Captivity of Babylon there had been, in whatever place Jews of the dispersion were congregated, meeting-houses where the books of the law were kept and matters pertaining to their religion could be discussed. These synagogues in the time of Jesus, when the temple worship was still the dominant feature of Hebraism, had even less of sanctity than attaches to them since the destruction of Jerusalem; they were used only on Sabbaths and commemorative occasions. All the treasures of religious association were still with the grass and the rain, the wild hills and the swelling of Jordan. Wealthy Jews had closets for personal devotions, rooms dedicated to reading and meditation, little kiosks on the housetops, looking toward Jerusalem; but in the crowded warrens of the poor there were no such privacies. Any man among them subject to visitation of the Spirit must have turned instinctively toward those places where of old God had visited Abraham, Elijah, and Isaiah. It is impossible not to conclude that to the circumstances of great light and space in which he received it, quite as much as to the compulsory co-operations and inter-dependence of poverty from which he came, we owe the spacious social character of the teaching of Jesus.

Above the plain of Gennesaret lie the orchards; first the olives with the vines between; above the olives the figs; above the figs the apricots, almonds, walnuts. Beyond the orchards the wild jungle begins — oak and thorn and terebinth; at last the "trees of God," spired fir and fan-spread cedar.

Here the charcoal-burner's hut would have sheltered him, or one of those low stone sheds used by the shepherds at lambing-time. At this latitude the sky retains its blueness on until midnight, the stars are not pricked in on one plane, but draw the eye to the barred door of space. A man praying here all night on one of these open hill-fronts might think he heard them swinging to their stations, might hear without any fancying, the heavy surge of the Mediterranean roll up along the western buttress of the Bridge. At dawn the fishing fleet would break out of the lake towns like doves out of a dove-cote, and caravans, starting early to avoid the heat of the day, begin to crawl along the *Wadi el Haman*. Hours such as this God flowed into him, filled and overfilled him.

And with all his being so filled and foaming with

the new wine of his gospel, he retained the shape
he had from the potter.

He was a small-town man and no world-builder.
He preached the Kingdom of God, knowing God for
a spirit and having an increasing realization of the
kingdom as a state of being. But he had no program. He followed the inward voice, and followed
it instinctively with the freedom of a river in its
natural channel, with no fretting of the flesh. But
where the voice left him uninformed he was simply
a man from Nazareth; his social outlook was the
outlook of a villager.

Formerly, great prophets of Israel had come out of
the Wilderness; their words were full of the terrible
things—thunders, earthquakes, fire on the mountains. But the words of Jesus are all of the small
town: the candle and the bushel, the housewife's
measure of yeast, the children playing in the street.
The rich he knew only as the poor and the oppressed
know them; the kings of his parables were the kings
of fairy-tale and legend, such kings and potentates
as make the stock of the village story-teller. His
very way of speaking was a folk way, the pithy
sentence, the pregnant figure. He saw God reflected
in every surface of the common life and taught in
parables which are, after all, but a perfected form of
the quizzes and riddles dear to the unlettered wit.
That is why so many of them are remembered while

his profounder sayings escaped his hearers. It is evident from the form of these, blunted as they are by retranslation, that they were, many of them, cast in the matched and balanced sentences of Hebrew verse, which accounts in part for their easy retention.

He was a man wise in life, but unlearned. He read no books but the scriptures; wrote nothing, took the folk way of transmitting his teaching from mouth to mouth and trusted God for the increase; and he had the folk way in his profoundest speech, of identifying himself with the Power that used him. He dramatized all his relations to the Invisible. With it all he was a Jew of the circumcision. He grew up beyond Judaism as a stalk of grain grows from its sheath, but never out of it. Always to his death, it was there about the roots of his life. At Capernaum, when the centurion had come to him, touching the illness of his servant, it had been thought necessary to explain that the soldier had been good to the Jews and had built them a synagogue. In the sending of his disciples he had explicitly directed them not to go into Samaria. His final illumination on this point he took with that extraordinary spiritual efficiency which distinguished him; equally with John the Baptist he understood that many should come in from strange lands and sit down with the children of Abraham and Isaac and Jacob. But the stalk had not yet overtopped its sheath when the returning twelve met him at the appointed rendezvous, which was probably Capernaum.

From what follows, one judges that the teaching of the disciples must have been attended with a measure of success. From this time on until he deliberately disappointed it, public expectation ran high. What with the coming and going, Jesus and the twelve were so beset that they found it necessary to withdraw some little distance out of the city along the lake shore, but the people marked where they went and, outrunning the boat, gathered about them again as sheep about a shepherd. Here, after he had preached to them, occurred one of those ebullitions of religious excitement which gave rise to the incident known as the miracle of the loaves and fishes. Popular enthusiasm is an excellent medium for miracle tales to ripen in. What probably happened was that the multitude were so fired by hope of the kingdom that they forgot their hunger and hung about until Jesus, having first dismissed his disciples toward Bethsaida upon the ship, sent them away. It was the plan, no doubt, to rejoin the twelve after he had refreshed himself on the mountain, as his custom was after any notable effort, by deep draughts of prayer. And along in the fourth watch of the night his disciples, being on the sea and the moon shining, saw him come walking on the water as though he would have passed them.   But they, thinking him a spirit, cried out in alarm until he spoke to them and came into the ship and comforted them.   So Mark sets down what he recalled of what Peter told him.

There was an earlier incident still of the crossing of this same lake, on the night before the healing of the demoniac which led to their being avoided by the cities of Gadara.   On that occasion a storm arose—one of those sudden flaws of wind whirling down from Hermon to be sucked into the Rift of Jordan.   They would spring up all in an instant, beating the lake from jade to blue and silver and then white with spume, and as suddenly die away again. But while the clumsy fishing-craft labored in the teeth of it Jesus slept until the boatmen, at the last gasp of their strength and skill, cried to him, "Master, help or we perish."   Immediately, when he was awakened, he said to them, "Why are ye fearful, O ye of little faith?" and also he said, "Peace, be still," and the wind fell off, and the ship righted.   All of which can be explained away by anybody who finds himself endowed with the kind of mind which demands it.   Did Peter really tell Mark that Jesus walked *on* the water or that he walked along it, along the shallow, tideless beach, so lost in meditation that it was not until they called to him from the boat, anchored a few feet offshore, that he was aware of

them? Had he been there all the night, walking by
the still waters, instead of on the mountain where
they supposed him? Peter should have known, but
certainly *if* he knew, it took more than a miracle of
walking on the water to keep Peter faithful at
the crisis at Jerusalem. After all, what a miracle
needs for its acceptance, is demonstration rather
than argument. We believe the miracles of healing because we have known of cures being accomplished in our own day, and we do not believe
in walking on the water, because it isn't done among
our acquaintances. Such incidents as these are told
of all prophets, as a symbol of the extension of their
powers over fields felt to be within man's province,
but as yet beyond his capacity.

What actually did happen was that the ship,
instead of making port at Bethsaida as had been
planned, was blown out of its course back to the
coast of Galilee. Here the very thing that Jesus
had sought to avoid at Capernaum awaited him. He
was immediately recognized and beset by the sick
borne in litters, and by throngs struggling only for
the touch of his garments. Many that touched him
were made whole by the faith that was in them, but
it is notable here that he is not said to have healed
anybody purposefully. From this time forth he
showed a tendency deliberately to avoid the work
of healing as an impediment to his preaching career.

There is a hint in the gospel narrative that at this juncture, when his popularity in the thickly populated plain of Gennesaret had reached its height, there was a tentative attempt to put him at the head of some sort of organized revolution, an attempt which he evaded. This would account for several things that followed in the interim between the return of the twelve and the journey up to Jerusalem. It accounts for the falling away of the disappointed populace, and for the secrecy which was maintained as to his movements afterward. He might have wished to avoid another popular demonstration, so uncomprehending, and his frequent trips across the border of Galilee might easily have been to escape the attention of Herod, who at this time certainly heard of him and began to wonder if this might not be John the Baptist come to life again to vex him.

About this time we read of Pharisees coming all the way from Jerusalem to see and question. They found for their first item that he and his disciples ate with unwashed hands; that is to say, that they omitted the ceremonial symbol of cleansing before meat. Attempting a rebuke, they found themselves rebuked in turn, and that roundly, convicted of lip service, of hypocrisy, of neglecting the commandments of God in favor of their traditions, making clean the outside of the cup and the platter, but inwardly full of ravening and wickedness. He cried woe unto them for the tithing of mint and cumin and passing over the judgment and the love of God; woe for that they loved the chief seats in the synagogue and greetings in the market. "Woe unto you scribes and Pharisees, hypocrites, ye are as graves which appear not, and men that walk over them are not aware of them!" So are they who are under the influences of Pharisees, defiled by unsuspected corruption.

And one of the lawyers, those whose business it was to draw out of the scriptures interpretations to suit the exigencies of his clients, said, "Master, saying this thou reproachest us also." And Jesus answering, said:

"Woe unto you also, ye lawyers . . . for you build sepulchers to the prophets, and your fathers killed them." With much more in the same strain to the effect that the blood of all the prophets should be required of their generation. "For," said he, referring to their method of distorting the scriptures to their advantage, "Ye have taken away the key of knowledge; ye entered not in yourselves"—into the understanding of God, he meant—"and those that were entering ye hindered."

Then he called the people to him and deliberately tore across the whole fabric of Levitical cleansing which held the theory and practice of Pharisaism together. Once for all he rid his name people of the accumulated tradition which reduced the process of daily living to a formula in the effort to avoid defiling or being defiled. "For there is nothing without a man," taught Jesus, "which entering into a man can defile him, but the things which come out of him . . . for out of the heart of men proceed evil thoughts . . . thefts, covetousness, deceit, lasciviousness . . . all these things come from within and defile a man."

It was a pronouncement which had effects far reaching in the organization of his followers after his death, and carried them beyond what Jesus himself found necessary; it became, in fact, the door through which the gospel passed to the Gentiles.

But he had struck at a very tender part in the armor of Pharisaical respectability, and from this time on he became the special mark of their animosity, seeking always to provoke him to the point at which the law might take hold of him. It had something to do, no doubt, with the privacy of his movements; though that would have found sufficient excuse in the wish to instruct and prepare his disciples for the work which now, by divine intuition, he saw shaping dimly before them. Leaving Bethsaida, he is heard of in the parts of Dalmanutha and in the borders of Magadan; he journeyed to Tyre and Sidon. Here he was in a region predominately Gentile and, until his return from Cæsarea-Philippi, out of the jurisdiction of Herod. He went unrecognized for the most part, and undeclared; but a man so marked as Jesus, attended by twelve who pay him the deepest attention and reverence, cannot always be hid. Near Dalmanutha Pharisees came forth again, this time demanding a sign. His disciples being of the masses and distrusting all aristocracies either of manners or morals, thought they came to tempt him, but Jesus understood them better. His scorn licked them like a flame, "Hypocrites, thinking to discern the sky and not able to read the signs of the times!" which showed that he had been reading them himself to some purpose; but to their wicked and adulterous generation no sign should be given, save the sign of the prophet Jonas, the sign of their own degeneracy which called for a signal handling from God. On two or three occasions during this journey, compassion broke down his reluctance to heal, though more than ordinary precautions were taken to prevent the healing from being known. It is notable that on these occasions, lacking the flux of a popular belief in him, he sometimes reinforced his method by symbolic touchings and an application to the eyeballs of the blind.

On his journey into Tyre and Sidon one incident preserved to us shows the gradual widening of his mind to the world outside of Jewry. In one of the

cities where he concealed himself he was recognized
by a Syrophœnician woman who would have had
him cast forth a devil out of her daughter. "But,"
said Jesus, "let the children first be filled; it is not
meet to take the children's bread and cast it unto
the dogs." There spoke the Nazarene and the
Hebrew, thinking of the chosen people. "Yea,
Lord," the woman answered him in his own figure,
"but the dogs under the table eat of the children's
crumbs." And the answer pleased him, for though,
as in the case of the centurion, he had not found
such faith in Israel, he honored it when he found it.

§

They would have been a month or two at this
business, holding on until late in November, if, as I
think, it was the advent of the early rains which
turned them east and south from Cæsarea-Philippi.
They passed over Ephraim; on the plains of Phœ-
nicia they smelled the sea. Toward Sidon they
heard it pounding, saw between the low coast hills
its white hands cast up. Hereabout they struck
into the great coast road passing between Surrepta
and Sidon, followed it as far as the gorge of Litany,
perhaps—for it is not stated that they entered into
either of the cities—and, climbing the sharp comb
of hills between that and the upper Jordan, dropped
down to Cæsarea-Philippi. For the most part it
was pleasant going, past high, well-watered valleys

and woods of maple, oak, and bay.   In the neighborhood of cities more Roman than Galilee they
saw instruments of ignominious execution set up,
and those melancholy processions . . . the criminal
bearing his cross, whipped forth by the soldiery,
and following afar off, the rabble, curious and
scoffing.

They would put in awhile at sequestered villages,
preaching perhaps, to such select few as were able
to hear the Word, and then to the road again, where
they slept at ancient khans, at shepherds' huts, and
many a night all open to the stars.   They ate such
food as they bought at the wayside, rough, wild figs
of the sycomore, and parched grain gleaned in the
fields.   They would sit Eastern fashion on the
ground, and, each making his little fire of the stalks,
and threshing out the scorched ear in the hand,
they would wash down the half-cooked grain with
wine from a goatskin bottle, while they talked of
things pertaining to the kingdom.   At the end of
the long twilight there would come a moment when,
with heads bowed and covered, there would run a
reverent murmur about the camp—*Hear, O Israel,
the Lord thy God is one Lord.* . . . The immemorial
declaration of the Shema.

Art has done too much for this man, to paint him
forever tried, scourged, forever a-dying.   He was
not only a man of the small towns, but of the hills,

the open road.   He is seen at his best here, striding
a little ahead of his companions, bronzed, hardy.
the turban off to catch the mountain coolness, the
long hair blown backward from the rapt countenance,
and over him a higher heaven than had yet lifted
upon man.   Of the twelve or fourteen months which
scholars allow to his ministry, how much of it was
spent out of cover!   At the preaching of John in
the Rift of Jordan, on the mount of the Wilderness,
in the hills back of Gennesaret, on the road to Cæsarea-Philippi, sleeping under the oaks at Gethsemane.
Nothing else accounts so readily for his preoccupa-
tion with the natural rather than the institutional
relations of men.

It was in this fashion he came to Philip's handsome capital.   Philip the Tetrarch was as much of
a Jew as a brother of Herod Antipas could be, and
Perea was a district counted to Israel, though its
influences were largely Greek.   The citadel, from
its rocky promontory, overlooks the wheat-fields
and the mulberry-trees of the upper Jordan valley.
Here full born from its basalt cavern, sacred to the
god of the Beast-in-man, springs Israel's sacred
river.   Close to the spot where the faith of the God-
in-man received its earliest formative impulse, still
it wets with its spray between the wild rose and the
honeysuckle, Pan's ancient altar.   It is not recorded
that Jesus entered Cæsarea-Philippi, but he remained

in the vicinity long enough to be recognized and sought for healing, and for the great change which had long been foreshadowed in the character of his ministry to reach its full development. For it was here that Jesus put to the twelve a question which must have been shaping in his own mind ever since the early summer, when John had first put it to him by the mouth of two of his own disciples.

"Whom do men say that I am?"

And they answered him: "John the Baptist. But some say Elias, and others, One of the Prophets." For it was always in the minds of Israel that the True-Speaking could pass in and out of Life and come again. Jesus held them steadily to the question.

"Whom say ye that I am?" And Peter, the impetuous, burst out with the faith that burned in him, "Thou art the Christ."

Then said Jesus, "Blessed art thou, Simon Barjona, for flesh and blood hath not revealed to thee, but my Father which is in Heaven."

It must have been here, and by the help of what he accepted as a revelation on the part of his disciples, that Jesus settled for himself much that must have seemed difficult and perplexing in his own experience. He had begun the preaching of the Kingdom of God at hand as a joyous certainty, a common heritage of the time, his only by a short priority of announcement. Feeling his knowledge of these things only a small part of what might be gathered up by any sincere soul who addressed himself to such discovery, he had come, as do all prophets and poets, to find it looked upon with suspicion by the multitude, a strange and singular thing, misunderstood and misrated.

As his revelation increased in him, together with his knowledge of the want of it in others, he saw even between himself and his chosen intimates a gulf immeasurable. It is at this point that genius falters. Sometimes in sheer terror of being alone with its message, it fails altogether, or weakly turns back to seek in human relations a surcease of strangeness. But Jesus, finding himself so much in advance of his time that twenty centuries have scarcely caught up with him, found himself unaffrighted because not wholly without direction. Woven out of the faith of his race, by a long line of prophets, the mantle of Messiahship waited for him who could fulfil it. It cannot be said that at any time until the very last day of his life Jesus publicly assumed it, but from this time forth he went clothed in the certainty of harmony between himself and the expectation of the ages. Though his time rejected him, he became a part of all times in as much as he was a figure of prophecy. The feeling of being prepared for and expected satisfied, for the man of Nazareth, that sense of *belonging*, the hunger for which frets great souls to their undoing.

That the incident stood both in his mind and that of his disciples for a definitely changed relationship appears at once. When he had charged them that they should make none of these things known, he began to teach them how it was that he should go up to Jerusalem, and what things he should suffer there. Certainly he must have carried these things in his mind for some time before he spoke of them; finding no way to reconcile them with his first joyous prevision of the kingdom, until he had accepted himself in the light of a fulfilment of prophecy. That his disciples found them utterly irreconcilable with any conception they had of him appears from Peter's hasty, "Far be it from thee, Lord; this shall not be unto thee." But even Peter, reminded in his turn that he smelled of the things of men rather than of God, could hardly have understood what followed. For Jesus, calling the people to him, and his disciples, also, said: "Whosoever will come after me, let him deny himself and take up his cross and follow me. For whosoever will save his life shall lose it; but whosoever shall lose his life for my sake and the gospel's, the same shall save it. For what shall it profit a man if he shall gain the whole world and lose his own soul? . . ."

Other things he said which, as they afterward re-

called, referred more explicitly to the fate which
was even then preparing for him. But it seems
hardly possible it could have been clearly indicated
or at all understood, for when the blow fell it found
them wholly unprepared. In the light of what occurred later, they harked back to interpret what he
had said. At the time, other things better remembered drove it from their minds.

Some days after Peter's ready declaration, Jesus
took him, together with James and John, high and
apart on the mountain for one of those sessions of
silent prayer to which he owed his spiritual suste-
nance.

Hermon draws up out of the plain of the upper
Jordan as the roots of a great oak lift out of the
ground. The land is filled with the sound of running waters; full-born rivers leap from limestone
caves and go roaring toward the Rift. The shrub
is close-leaved here; at intervals great trees stand
up; they reach the borders of perpetual snows.

On this occasion the little company must have
climbed up beyond the tree-line into the region of
the stony waste before Jesus drew aside for his hour
of communion. Wearied sooner at their own devotions, humbly his disciples watched him. While
he prayed they saw the fashion of his countenance
change, grow white and shining, and a bright cloud
overshadowed them. These were very simple souls

to whom undreamed-of things may happen. While
Jesus was wrapt from himself did a white flash of
his burning spirit strike across to them? Such things
are possible. Or was it the alpen glow, that most
transcendent of all the visible manifestations of God,
flooding down from Hermon, touching all things with
its divine transfiguration? They were fishermen of
the low, lake region to whom the stained air laving
the peaks of the mountains was as strange as splendid. It spoke to them as all beauty of nature speaks
to the devout, of God. Bathed in it, they saw their
Messiah as it became all true Jews to see him, radi-
ant between the Law and the Prophets, in the
figures of Moses and Elias.

Coming down from the heights, touched with awe
of the celestial wonder, they ventured a timid question. "Why," said they, "do the Scribes say that
Elias should come first?" For if this was truly the
Christ of prophecy, there wanted somewhat to the
fulfilment.

Said Jesus, "Elias is already come, but they knew
him not and did unto him whatsoever they listed."
By which they understood him to refer to John the
Baptist. More is reported of the same character,
but all too much colored by what happened in the
interval between the writing and the recording to
be veridical. It is enough, however, to define the
path by which their thoughts traveled to the idea

of Jesus and his teaching which finally possessed them.

There was a longer road still, in which they were to reconcile the person of the crucified carpenter with the glorious figure of the Messiah limned upon the Hebrew consciousness, but from this time forth we see Jesus held to the perfect poise by the knowledge of what God expected of him.   He was not the first man nor the last to perish for the Word, but this was unique in him, that he never doubted nor repented.   And if he saw in himself the fulfilment of prophecy, the Anointed one of Israel, who shall gainsay him?   If he was not the Messiah the Jews expected, he was at least the only one they ever had.

And it shall come to pass when he has brought
    low everything that is in the world,
And has sat down in peace for the age on the throne
    of his kingdom,
Then joy shall be revealed,
And rest shall appear!

Then healing shall descend in dew,
And disease shall withdraw,
And anxiety and anguish and lamentation pass from
    amongst men,
And gladness proceed through the whole earth.

And wild beasts shall come forth from the forest
    and minister unto men,
And asps and dragons shall come forth from their
    holes to submit themselves to a little child.

And it shall come to pass in those days that the reaper
    shall not grow weary,
Nor those that build be toilworn,
For the works shall of themselves speedily advance,
Together with those who do them in much tran-
    quillity.

[From the *Apocalypse of Baruch*, a Jewish work of the last
half of the first century, which strongly influenced the style
of the synoptic gospels.]

VI

AND if not the Messiah of expectation, how then
did he succeed in fulfilling the prophecy without satisfying the dream? His message he knew to
be Messianic, but that he himself fell short in some
particulars of the long-cherished ideal seems to be
indicated in the last clause of the message he sent
to John, "Blessed is he that finds no occasion of
stumbling in me." Here we see the man from
Nazareth imposing his Levitical training on the
prophet. Thus and so Messiah was to come; and
yet here was the saving Word delivered in quite
other ways.

The one feature irreconcilable between the inheritance and the revelation of Jesus was the estab-
lishment of the kingdom. This was to be the work
of the Messiah, and it is probable that when Jesus
began to preach his early coming—before they had
gone through the cities of Israel—he was thinking
of a person quite apart from himself. The growth
of the idea that he himself was the fulfilment of
prophecy was shown in him; it did not reach him
much in advance of the certainty that if he was to

restore the kingdom to Israel, it was not to be in his
own time and his own flesh.   He was to prepare for
it by revealing the true nature of the Father and
establishing kinship between God and man.   He
was to reorganize the thoughts and affections of
men in the Spirit and in Love.   But more and more
as he felt on all sides the pressure of Roman empiry,
of established governmental and economic systems,
he realized the necessity of breaking up the mold
of society, of pouring its fluid stuff into lines more
in conformity with his revelation of Brotherhood in
man.   To speak in our tongue, Jesus accepted the
idea of social revolution without any clear notion
of how it was to be accomplished.   The entrance
of the individual into the kingdom was a matter
of personal spiritual regeneration, to which Jesus
held the key.   The setting up of the great commandment as a human institution, lay in a region
beyond the reach of his most poignant revelation.

But again, this was to be the work of the Messiah,
and if Jesus were the Christ, then his work somehow,
in some fashion.   And Jesus was to die.   Of this he
seems to have been certain from Cæsarea-Philippi
forward;   intimations of his end thickened as the
time drew on.   Casting about for the solution of
these apparently irreconcilable conditions, he fixed
upon the common belief in the return of the prophets.
How readily Israel could accept such passage in and

out of death is seen in their question about John the
Baptist. John was Elias and Jesus was John come
again. And if Jesus were Christ, why should not
a second coming, not in the flesh, but with Power,
show forth the wonders that the first had missed?
In some such fashion the man from Nazareth worked
out his incompleted revelation.

Something had been accomplished by the tempo-
rary withdrawal of Jesus from the cities of Gennesaret. Once for all he had cleared himself from any
movement which had for its objective the taking of
the kingdom of heaven by violence. His work of
healing was definitely relegated to a secondary place.
Disappointed of this transitory hope, the rabble fell
away, but many sincere souls still resorted to him.

One phrase from an incident at Cæsarea-Philippi
lights up for us, as by a spark struck from a common
experience, the state of mind of the devout of Israel,
"Lord, I believe, Help thou mine unbelief." It was
the cry that had burst with tears from the father of
the dumb demoniac whom the disciple could not
heal. Coming down from the mount of transfiguration, Jesus had found a crowd gathered about the
remnant of his disciples, and in their midst the man
begging relief for his son. It was not until the Master accosted him with the customary formula,
"Believest thou that I canst do this thing?" that the
deep-seated doubt came to the surface in that cry.

So Israel, unhealed by all its prophets, voiced its doubt and its desire. Upon this cry the common faith tossed to and fro, rallied, broke, and scattered, came to fulfilment at last in martyrdom long after he had passed. At times his human nature shook its shadow over the surface of his mood. He was impatient with the incompetence of his disciples. . . . "O faithless generation, how long shall I suffer you!" He pronounced woe on Chorazin and Bethsaida. At times a wistful humanness broke through. "Can it be that a prophet shall perish from Jerusalem!"

Not that there wanted occasions to try the patience of the teacher. No sooner had the disciples been given leave to think of Jesus as the Messiah than they were found, on the way back from Cæsarea-Philippi, in fact, disputing who should be greatest. A man discovered casting out devils in the name of Jesus was forbid by them because he was not of their following. To both of these, especially to the latter—first instance of the independent spread of his teachings during his life—Jesus made answer and illustration so unequivocal that it is a mystery how his name people have so long avoided both. "For whosoever shall give a cup of cold water in my name hath done it unto me . . . " he said, touching the question of unauthorized healing, and left them in no doubt as to the quality of their offense against "one of these lesser ones who believe in me." But the millstone hangs still about the neck of the church, because of what it has done to those who take the name of Jesus in some fashion other than their own.

Incidents such as these, showing how far his chosen disciples were from comprehending him, contributed to the sense of disappointment voiced in his invective against the cities of Galilee. . . . "For if the mighty works which have been done in thee had been done in Tyre and Sidon, they would have repented in sackcloth and ashes." It had its part in the urge which drove him, knowing what awaited him there, to set his face steadily toward Jerusalem.

This would have been two or three months before Passover, nearer if we accept the incident of the temple tax which was collected in Capernaum. The rains would have been well on, the winter wheat was up, and as many as were able making ready for the yearly pilgrimage. Altogether an excellent time to waken men to the immanence of the kingdom.

Concerning the manner of this journey, there is little said but much indicated. It was traveled with a considerable company, augmenting as they went, Jesus and the twelve with some members of their families, and certain women who ministered to them, Mary of Magdala, out of whom were cast seven devils, and some others. They went afoot, with perhaps a donkey or two for the slender luggage; and every mile they trod was historic holy ground. It was the custom, on approaching a village where Jesus would teach, for two or three of the disciples to go ahead and make such provision as they could for the entertainment of the Master, announcing him, and no doubt appointing a place where he could be heard. But there must have been many occasions between villages or in those which proved inhospitable, when they camped happily in the fields or in the courtyard of the wayside khans. It appears that a first attempt was made to reach Jerusalem by the ancient Egyptian road which ran through Samaria, past Sychar and the vale of Shechem, but the Samaritans would not receive them. At the first village where the inhabitants proved unfriendly, the sons of Zebedee would have called down fire upon them after the manner of Elijah, so hardly had they learned the lesson that the Son of Man was come to save and not to destroy. The Samaritans, always an easy, idol-loving people, closer to Rome under the hand of the Procurator Pontius Pilate, and furthest from the national dream, pushed their indifference to the prophet to the prohibitive point, for we hear no more of Jesus having set foot in the country of Shechem. They returned, instead, and approached Jerusalem from the south- east by way of the other side of Jordan.

It was in the bitterness of this rejection, no doubt, that he said to one who would have followed him, "Foxes have holes . . . but the son of man hath not where to lay his head." And to another who made excuse that he must first bury his father, "Let the dead bury their dead," since dead he found them in the spirit. So they passed to the parts of Syria beyond the Bridge from which, when the Bridge was broken under the heel of the Roman legionaries, the tide of Islam rolled in upon them.

This is a high, level country with a wind always in the wheat and great oaks rustling along the ridges. In Gilead there is balm, fields of fragrant herbs, orchards of pomegranate and apricot. Moab is a land of pastures; the roadways are beaten to dust by the flocks; toward Amman herds of camels feeding. A band of pilgrims passing from city to city of the Greek league of the Decapolis would seldom be far from the sound of the shepherds' pipes and the heavy bells of the cattle as they break down the *wadis* to the drinking-places. This was the land of Gad and Reuben, and, though strong in Greek influence, was still predominantly Hebrew. Scarcely had the apostolic band set foot in it when they were met by Pharisees with the customary Levitical quibble.

This time it was an inquiry as to whether it was lawful for a man to put away his wife for every reason.   In Jewry the power of divorce lay in the hands of the husband, requiring scarcely more than the mere form of saying so to make it lawful.   It is possible that the party of the Pharisees were honestly opposed to the abuses which had sprung up under Roman laxness, but it is also probable that they were not unwilling to set Jesus at odds with Herod, who, in the thick of his troubles between Herodias and the father of his wife, was sensitive on the subject of divorce.   If he had beheaded John for his strictures, what might he not be provoked to undertake against the man from Nazareth?   Jesus, however, with his customary tact, avoided the personal issue and maintained the stand he had earlier taken of inviolable marriage, basing it not upon any Levitical revelation, but as is inevitable, upon the natural mating habits of humankind "as it was in the beginning."   Here, too, is the first recognition of human expedient; "because of the hardness of your hearts," divorce was allowed by Moses.   Which did not, however, render less obligatory the single, lifelong relation, for though polygamy was still to be found, it appears nowhere to have crossed his horizon nor to have entered into the problem of early Christianity.   In this connection one may speak of the sole other incident which illuminated for us, in the light of the teachings of Jesus, the vexed relations of sex.   This is an incident which finds its

way into no canonical writing until the early part
of the second century, when it was inserted in the
document attributed to John, where, in spite of
some exegetical difficulties, it makes good its claim
to consideration. It is placed in the vicinity of
Jerusalem, and by tradition wholly unsupported, but
of high antiquity, connected with the person of Mary
of Magdala. By those of the priestly party, who
hoped to catch him tripping, there was brought to
him a woman taken in adultery. But Jesus, making
as though he heard them not, stooping, wrote with
his finger upon the ground, and when they continued asking what should be done to her, lifted himself at last, inquiring of them the penalty. Whereupon her accusers insisted that it was lawful she
should be stoned. Said Jesus, "Let him that is
without sin among you first cast a stone." In this
fashion he went the first mile which they compelled
him. But when at the end of the second he found
himself alone with the woman, he left off writing to
say, "Hath no man condemned thee?"

Said she, "No man, Lord."

Then said Jesus: "Neither do I condemn thee.
Go, sin no more."

Words and acts, they are both of a piece with all
that we know of Jesus; for was he not among the
prophets and given to symbolic acts charged with
more than mere words conveyed? Writing in the

dust was it not to say—for we do not know if he
had really learned to write at all—even so is this
sin of which you accuse her, written in the body,
which, being dust, perishes? Whether or not the
incident occurred as stated, it goes with the answer
to the Pharisees to show, that though Jesus constituted chastity a matter of mind as well as body,
he made no more of lapses from it than of other sins,
and forgave them as readily. He put the desire of
the flesh on exactly the same moral footing as the
greed of wealth and the lust of pride, neither con-
demning it more severely, as the church has done,
nor more easily excusing, as is the way of the world.

It is doubtful, however, if the twelve grasped anything of the breadth of his comment on the existing
law, allowed by Moses because of "the hardness of
their hearts," for we find them moving in an orbit
as narrow almost as that of his detractors, forbid-
ding the children which were brought to him to
be blessed, and still unlessoned when he, taking a
little child in his arms and setting him in the midst
of them, declared that of such were the kingdom
of heaven. In a very little while, here are the sons
of Zebedee, at the first opportunity asking for the
chief seats in heaven.

This takes us back a little to one of the earlier
incidents of the Perean pilgrimage, to the young man
who had kept all the law and the commandments

from his youth up, and was still concerned as to how
he might inherit eternal life. Said the teacher:
"One thing thou lackest . . . sell all thou hast . . .
take up thy cross and follow me." But to the disciples, after the young man had gone away grieving
(for he had great possessions), Jesus said, "How
hardly shall a rich man enter into the kingdom."

"And," says Mark, "the disciples were astonished at his words."

This is more important even than the saying.
They were astonished. For eight or nine months
they had been with him, preaching preparation for
the kingdom, and this was the first they had heard
of personal wealth as a bar to entry; a serious over-
sight on the part of the Master, if we are to read
this comment on the particular case as constituting
an essential doctrine. All through the Galilean
ministry not a word has been heard of it, though
Luke expressly tells us that there were women of
substance in his train. Later, in Jerusalem, we find
him accepting the use of a room for the Passover,
and a garden without the walls, from those of his followers whose fortunes permitted of such lendings.
It appears, however, not only from circumstances
such as these, but from what immediately follows,
that it was not the possession of riches which Jesus
discredited, but the attachment to them; for he
goes on to put in the same category, brethren and

sisters, parent or wife or children. Just as curt had
been his rejection of one who would have been his
disciple, but wished first to bury his father. The
stress upon wealth, as against other distractions to
the spirit, is ours, not Jesus'.

Too much has been made of the incident of the
rich young man and of a later parable of Lazarus
and Dives, which illustrated a popular notion,
pagan as well as Hebrew, that somehow in its turning the wheel of life must bring to every soul the
full round of experience—to the poor riches, and to
the rich poverty, and to those that mourned rejoicing. Something of this kind must have been in the
mind of the disciples, for though this seems to have
been the first time that Jesus' doctrine of self-
abnegation came clear to them, it set them off immediately in the direction of the logical compensa-
tion. Something of tenderness for the Master's
disappointment in the rich young man—for Jesus,
beholding him, had loved him—must have been in
Peter's, "Lo, *we* have left all and followed thee."
But nothing could have illustrated so completely the
gap which in spite of all this intimate fellowship, lay
between Jesus and his disciples, as the way in which
James and John turned the promise of spiritual re-
ward with which Jesus met the profferred consola-
tion, into a hope of material advancement. It was
not long before they found a naïve expression for it.

It seems that while they were on the way to Jerusalem the reserve and caution which had characterized the movement of the Master for the past few months were suddenly laid aside. Jesus resumed the leadership, walked openly at the head of his disciples, filled with power. In answer to their fear and amazement he must have tried again to prepare them for what was to happen shortly at Jerusalem, and again the revelation was either too symbolic to be clear or too clear to be believable. All that they seem to gather from it was that the expected apocalypse was at hand, and, full of unshakable confidence in the result, James and John preferred their request. It was very simply that they might sit the one on the right hand, the other on the left, of him in glory.

Said the Master: "Ye know not what ye ask. Can ye drink of the cup that I drink of and be baptized with the baptism that I am baptized with?" They thought they could, knowing nothing of what the words signified, thinking of them, no doubt, as purely material, and that death and humiliation could in no wise be endured by one who healed lepers and raised the dying by the hand. But it was not their obtuseness which touched Jesus so nearly, nor the jealousy of the other ten at their asking, as the evidence of self-seeking, the utter failure of his disciples to grasp the teaching which the last phases of his life were so completely to exemplify—the need and the power of service. "For whoso seeketh his life shall lose it and he that loseth shall find . . . and whosoever will be chief among you, let him be the servant of all . . . for the son of man came not to be ministered unto but to minister."

§

Of the recorded part of this Perean pilgrimage there is very little more except what is common to all his ministry. Of healings there was but one—a blind man by the roadside as they came into Jericho; of parables the same sort, and perhaps the same that belonged to the preaching in Galilee. They were all of the kingdom and how it should be constituted, and of the Fatherliness of God. The kingdom of heaven was a net which was let down into the sea; it was a field of sown wheat among which the enemy scattered tares; it was the leaven hid in three measures of meal. It was anything that might imply separation of what is good from what is evil, the deliberate choice of the soul. The kingdom was something which, when you had found it, was worth all that you had to pay, into possession of which you might not enter without the full price. It was a little child whom he had set in their midst and said "such is the kingdom of heaven." It was in being all that the child was, trusting, doing no evil, thinking none, all-loving, glad. The kingdom of heaven proceeded from the heart outward and was not affected by material observances. It was the faith of the mustard-seed, which, by merely accepting the condition of being a seed and growing, became as a tree in the branches of which lodged the birds of the air. "And behold, the kingdom of God is within you."

Of God there was less to say because simpler. He was a father pitying his children, rejoicing more over one sinner which repented than over ninety-and-nine which went not astray. He was the just judge and the wise master; the friend of the soul of man. He heard prayer and answered it, and men ought always to pray and to faint not.

As to what Jesus said of himself there is less than this generation realizes. Nursed in an interpretation of Christianity which made Jesus the chief part of his own teaching, we have much to forget before we can see how apart he held himself from his doctrine. That day in Nazareth, when among his own kin he stood up in the synagogue and read from the book of Isaiah, was his first and only public attempt to represent himself as the fulfilment of prophecy. He read:

The spirit of the Lord is upon me, because he anointed me to preach good tidings to the poor . . . to proclaim the acceptable year of the Lord. But there is no evidence that when he began to say, "This day is the scripture fulfilled in your ears," that he thought of himself as anything more than the scripture described—an appointed preacher, another voice in the wilderness.   To John, who sent asking, he offered not himself, but his works.   Once in the press at Capernaum a woman cried out, "Blessed be the womb that bore thee and the breasts that gave thee suck."   And he answered her, rebukingly, "Rather blessed be they that hear the word of God and keep it."   And on the mountain, "Why call ye me Lord, Lord, and do not the things that I say?"

It was in some such frame as this that he passed through Perea for the last time and came again to the borders of Judea.

§

Of the unwritten part of this journey it is possible to think that much can be traced in the life of the Christian community during the next half-score of years.   How many were with him on the whole journey and how many joined him in the Rift of Jordan can only be conjectured, but he arrived in Jerusalem with a sufficient company of his Galilean friends to give to their intercourse a certain definite stamp.   Here was the beginning of that strong sense of community interest, the shared bread, the daily worship, grace before meat,—habits

of living which characterized the first proselyting
period of the new faith; the public testimony, the
benediction, the hymn-singing.   Above all, the gra-
cious kindliness, the cheer, the contained and quiet
joy which was shed as a savor from early Christian
behavior.   Such as they were he must have been—
little vessels all of them overfilled at his fountain.
*(By the watercourses of Reuben, great were the resolves
of heart!)*

Here, too, must have been established that acceptance of women in the Father, so unequivocal
that all Paul's prejudice could not afterward con-
trovert it; Jesus admitted them to argument, he
permitted them to sit in privileged places.   It does
not appear that he anywhere expressed himself as
opposed to any of the current notions of sex in-
feriority; rather to conduct himself as if he had not
known such distinctions to exist.   He had not one
manner for the virtuous housewife and another for
the woman of the town.   He yielded to the argument of the Syrophœnician woman, and in a story
told by John, which seems to be compounded of a
half-remembered parable and some items of actual
incident, he is shown revealing himself quite simply
to a woman at a wayside well, a woman of the despised Samaritan sect, thought to be so far outside
the grace of God as to be disbarred from the temple,
but not beyond the reach of his gospel.

Not wholly authenticated, but true enough to the situation to have been true in fact, is an incident related in the book of Apostolic Ordinances. There had arisen, it appears, in the primitive church, the question of a separate ministry for women, for among the Jews women had never been admitted to the highest intimacies of religion. John was strongly for it, urging that there had been no women present at the last supper, whereat Mary was seen to smile. But when Martha called their attention to it she denied that she had laughed, "For," said she, "he told us beforehand when he taught, that the weak should be saved through the strong." Whether or not the incident occurred as related, the freedom of Jesus from every form of social prejudice was evident enough to pull the early church about from its Oriental bias toward the subordination of women, and face it definitely to the larger liberty of the West. Themselves in bondage to the habit of their upbringing, the women of his following probably took less than he would have allowed them; it is not recorded that he ever refused any one of them what she asked. He included them, good and bad, in that democracy of the spirit which established a minimum value for every soul of both sexes and all classes.

§

At the time the little company came down out of the high, veiled land of Moab, all Jewry was

afoot and astir in this business of the Passover.   In
the month Adar the temple tax was collected, roads
were mended, sepulchers whitened lest any pilgrim
suffer defilement.   From every village a devoted
band set forth; the poor on their own feet, the rich
in litters; Jews of the dispersion; Alexandrine bank-
ers riding on camels.   All the stony lanes were
choked with bleating lambs for the Paschal rite,
heifers for sacrifice, vendors of doves moving under
great pyramids of cages.   Caravans went up—goods
of Damascus, Egyptian dates, silks of Arabia.
Every morning found hordes of market gardeners
with their donkeys waiting for the opening of the
gates.   Great loads of palm branches, of green
boughs cut from the jungle along Jordan, went in
for the building of booths.   In their gardens outside
the city the rich set up pavilions—for there were
no gardens within the holy city, lest the blown dust of
manure defile the temple—and relived from Sabbath to Sabbath the years their fathers spent in the
Wilderness.

Herod went up, needing greatly the public con-
sent to his war with Aretas, and the countenance
of the Roman authorities; Pontius Pilate, from his
official seat at Cæsarea-by-the-sea, new Roman
officials keen for this strange new festival, legionaries for the policing of the city.   A million and a
half—in favored years two million—pilgrims gathered

in Jerusalem. It was the time of the year's resurrection; the orchards budded, the tufted grass was greening, cyclamen came up in the clefts of the rock with round, shining leaves like shields of silver. Along the hard, white ways between the thorny hedges there was sound of psalm-singing.

Into all this pageantry of historical and religious observance Jesus came with his company, knowing the way he was to walk and able to walk in it. At the ford of Jordan, probably the same at which he was baptized, he was met by warning advices. "Depart hence. Herod will kill thee." To which he made answer, "Go tell that fox that to-day and to-morrow I cast out devils and do cures, and the third day I am perfected." A cryptic saying to his disciples, but if we read "finished" for perfected, clearly indicating that he knew his work so near an end that it was now immaterial what Herod should do to him. So with full courage he crossed over Jordan and stopped at Jericho, the fragrant. It sits in the midst of orchards close under the bluffs of Judea, having the glittering surface of the Dead Sea always on the south and the brown river flowing past. When the wind is right, blown gusts of the temple music come faintly down from Jerusalem, fifteen miles away. Here he spent the night and perhaps a Sabbath.

Two incidents, slight in themselves, illuminate

the public mind. He was addressed by a blind man as Son of David, and Zaccheus, the publican, climbed a tree that he might have a good look at the new prophet in the midst of the crowd that came out to meet him. For the movements of Jesus were noted; and to others than his immediate circle had spread the hope in him as the Messiah.

The road from Jericho to Jerusalem leads up a red gorge and its winding ridges, a hot, heavy way, blind, waterless. It figures chiefly as the scene of a parable which Jesus laid there, in which the falling among thieves was the likeliest, and the rescue by the good Samaritan the loveliest, that might have happened there. By this time there must have been a considerable company in the train of the man from Nazareth, traveling in a state of hardly suppressed excitement, for, says Luke, "They thought that the kingdom of God should immediately appear." They came singing, as befitted pilgrims, a song of going up, "songs of degrees," dating from the return from captivity.

I will lift up mine eyes unto the hills,

they sang, seeing the hill of Zion in the mind's eye long before they came in sight of it, and also

I was glad when they said unto me
Let us go into the house of the Lord!
Our feet shall stand within thy gates, O Jeru-
salem!

for it was a great commemorative occasion, and there were many in that company who had not yet seen that most moving sight to any Jew, the holy city.

They would have been all the morning climbing up out of the sweltering Rift to the cool ridges. At Bethpage, where the road to Bethany turns off from the main highway, they took their nooning. Just around the shoulder of Olivet they would have had the first glimpse of Jerusalem. It burst upon them, transfigured in the slant afternoon light, a city walled up to heaven from the gulfs of Hinnom and Kidron. First they saw the citadel, then the white towers of Antonia, the gilded temple roofs, and the long arcade of Solomon's porch wreathed for the festival . . . *whither the tribes go up, the tribes of the Lord unto the testimony of Israel, to give thanks unto the name of the Lord.* . . . And, looking on it, Jesus wept.

We can only conclude that what followed was born of the inspiration of the moment; it was part of that impassioned cry, "O Jerusalem, Jerusalem, how often would I have gathered thy children together!" which burst from him with all the warm and patriotic sentiment the sight of it stirred up, and with the knowledge deep in his own mind of what it was still to do to a prophet of Nazareth.

Perhaps the passage from Zacharia had just flashed upon his mind, "*Thy king shall come to thee, lowly and*

riding upon an ass. . . ." Jerusalem that dreamed
of a Messiah sitting in the heavens, clothed in authority; Jerusalem that stoned the prophets should
have a parable in the true prophetic manner, after
the fashion of Isaiah, who walked three years bare-
foot without his upper garment, and of Zedekiah,
who bound horns upon his forehead with which to
push against the Syrians.   Sending back to the village which they had just passed to borrow an ass
which he had seen tied there—for there were beasts
everywhere to be hired for the sight-seeing—Jesus
came riding on it into the chief city of the Jews, a
man of the masses, travel-stained, with long hair
like a woman's.

So he fulfilled, for those who strained after these
things, the strained letter of the prophecy.   Viewed
in any other light than that subtle spiritual irony
of which he was master, the incident takes on a poor
touch of human futility, and neither vanity nor
futility had any place in him.   To the simple Galileans, his followers, it appealed as an assumption of
new dignities.   They spread their garments before
him, raising a loud Hosanna.   From the temple
porch across Kidron came an answering shout.   It
was caught up by the crowd in the street, and many
curious and devout, who had listened to him in
Galilee and Perea, came pouring out of the eastern
gate, waving palms and welcoming:

Blessed be he that cometh in the name of the Lord!
Oh, give thanks unto the Lord, for he is good!

chanted the pilgrim band, and from the crowd streaming from the city gates came the antiphonal response:

For his mercy endureth for ever!

for so it was customary to receive pilgrims at the feast of the Passover. Throughout the capital it became known that the new prophet from Nazareth had arrived with his following.

Popular excitement must have died down very soon after the procession entered by the Eastern Gate. It tailed out in the narrow streets and lost itself in the vast throngs of the indifferent and merely curious. Nothing whatever happened. The diminishing band of enthusiasts made their way toward the temple, packed with the Jews of all Nations. It would have been about the hour of the evening sacrifice, the money-changers would have folded their tables, the vendors of doves had left for the day, the crowd was hushed and worshipful. Jesus and his handful of Galileans looked about on all the solemn wonders, and at evening retired to the village of Bethany.

The Lord is my strength and song
  And he is become my salvation.
The voice of rejoicing and salvation
  Is in the tabernacles of the righteous.
The right hand of the Lord doeth valiantly.

The right hand of the Lord is exalted,
  The right hand of the Lord doeth valiantly.

I shall not die but live,
  And declare the works of the Lord.
The Lord hath chastened me sore
  But he hath not given me over unto death.
Open to me the gates of righteousness,
  I will go into them, I will give thanks unto the
    Lord.

. . . .

I will give thanks unto thee, for thou hast answered
    me,
  And art become my salvation.
The stone which the builders rejected
  Is become the head of the corner.

This is the Lord's doing;
  It is marvelous in our eyes.
This is the day the Lord hath made;
  We will rejoice and be glad in it.
Save now, we beseech thee, O Lord;
  O Lord, we beseech thee, send now prosperity.

[Part of the *Hallel* sung at the end of the Paschal supper.]

VII

CONSIDER the lair of the lion of Judah, how it is established on the prongs of the great central plateau, walled up to heaven. On Zion is the citadel, Moriah is pieced out by solid piers of masonry to make room for the temple. Between them the tyropeon, the place of the merchants, leads down to Hinnom; round the eastern base sweeps the Valley of Jehoshaphat, through which flows Kidron. Gardens lie thick in the trough of Jehoshaphat and Hinnom, but the ravine at the back of the city is called Gehenna, for rubbish is thrown there and a fire for ever consumes the city's slough and waste. Across Kidron rises the Mount of Olives, from which the land falls eastward by terraces to the valley of the shadow, which is Jordan. Always Jerusalem looks into the gulf, but never quite to the bottom of it, and east away the blue hills of Moab float upon the horizon and affect the imagination like the sea. Northward stretches the hill country of Judea, full of contour and color. Reasons like these as much as history, have to do with the pride of Jerusalem and its fierce resentment of overlordship. Herod the Great being in part a Jew, held it with a strong, cruel hand; Archelaus could not hold it at all; and Pontius Pilate, at this time Procurator, lost it.

But before Rome took her, the worst had already happened to Jerusalem. She had fallen into the hands of the hierarchy. Political imposition is a yoke upon men's necks, but the rule of priests is a fetter to the understanding. When Pilate ordered the Roman standards into the city, standards bearing the image of the Emperor and hence an abomination, the Sanhedrin opposed him and won; when he set up votive shields in Herod's palace the four sons of Herod headed the protest to Rome; when he spent the temple treasure on an aqueduct he had the whole priestly party against him; but when a man came freely speaking his opinion of priests and the conduct of the temple, they made of the Procurator the instrument of his destruction. Whether they fought Pilate or used him, the mainspring of action was always the preservation of their Levitical authority.

Probably they thought they were right—it is one of the prime necessities of men in large numbers that they should think so of themselves—but one thing they knew, and that was that it was profitable. Here we touch on one other factor of the Hebrew religion which determined the development of Christianity as the soil on which it is reared determines

the harvest. We have seen how Jesus rooted himself in the reality of moral principle; all that follows
goes to show how the survival of his teaching was
shaped by the profound Hebrew conviction of the
efficacy of sacrifice. The pagan gave to his gods
when there was need or when he felt happy, but
Israel gave also because there was virtue in giving.
He gave whether God saved or destroyed him; he
gave more or less as God prospered him—the one
essential was that he should keep on giving. Israel
took up the principle of sacrifice, which is an indeter-
minate element of all religion, and made it over
with the aid of the business instinct.

What had been revealed to Judah as the soul's
supremest need had become a system. It was no
longer sacrifice, but tribute. As a people, Jews had
spread over the known world, but the heart of Jewry
still beat at Jerusalem; it was the one place where
offering was acceptable to the Lord. Wherever a
faithful Jew was found, from him to the temple
trickled a thin stream of gold. It came from Rome
and Egypt and Babylonia; it came even from a
prophet in Galilee and his twelve disciples. That
Jesus very clearly distinguished between tribute
and sacrifice is evident from the remark credited to
him on the payment of the temple tax. Tribute was
a thing which might be exacted of strangers, but
never of the Children; between them and the Father

no such necessity existed.   Nevertheless, he released
one of his disciples to go a-fishing to raise the money,
that no offense might be given.   He conformed to
the custom rather than, by raising an issue, delay a
greater matter; but his attitude toward the abuses
growing out of the system brooked no compromise.

The abuses were precisely those which a few centuries later sprang up among his name people; for
Israel had hit upon the one plan by which a hierarchy
may be consistently maintained, and Christianity,
blindly led by the blind, fell into the same ditch.
Whether it is called tribute or modernly disguised as
"systematic giving," it is only where sacrifice ceases
to be the soul's highest voluntary function and becomes a habit, that the priesthood attains to temporal power.   The constant flow of tribute into
Jerusalem had begotten a ring of grafters as invincible and corrupt as ever controlled a modern mu-
nicipality.   There were officials for collecting tribute
and for transmitting it, merchants of exchange who
sat in the temple porch to exchange coin of all
countries for the temple half-shekel, paying heavily
for the privilege.   There were inspectors of beasts
bought for sacrifice, who had to be compounded;
vendors of temple wares—incense, phylacteries,
reliquaries, such things as are sold immemorially
about temples.   Altogether the temple rake-off
amounted to about forty thousand dollars yearly.

All this was organized and in a measure controlled
by one Annas, ex-high priest, with his five sons,
priests all, and Caiphas, his son-in-law, high priest
for the current occasion.

How much of this was known to Jesus and his
disciples in Galilee is a matter of conjecture. Between affairs at the capital and the mass of the
people stood the sect of the Sadducees, adroit, worldly,
deriving authority solely from the books of Moses,
discrediting the prophets; they intrigued alike with
Rome and the priesthood, feathering their own
nests. Not unknown to Jesus, they drew less of
his condemnation than the Pharisees by making
fewer pretensions. It is probable, however, that the
Galileans had heard a rumor of these things as villagers hear them, things which they felt themselves
knowing to believe, or virtuous in denying. That
nothing was farther from their thoughts on the second morning, when they walked in from Bethany,
can be easily gathered from what followed.

Jesus had spent the night at the house around
which lingers the tradition of Martha, careful about
many things, and Mary, who chose the better part
in choosing to hear of the Kingdom. Bethany lies
on the Jordan side of Olivet, hid from the city;
Bethpage is at the junction on the Bethany road
with the great public highway; from here is one continuous suburb of hamlet and garden to the foot of

the rock from which the city soars above the abyss.
It is from this point that the temple first engaged
the eye, shining with the morning. From pillared
court within court it rose, dazzling, roofed with gold.
The smoke of the morning sacrifice went up; they
heard the choir chanting. But within, beyond the
court of the Gentiles, within the court of the Men
of Israel, which rose tier by tier from the court of
the Women, beyond the holy place where stood the
great altar, the Holy of Holies was empty, quite
empty.

This would have been Monday by the most reliable chronology. If they arrived at the temple in
the hour after the morning sacrifice before the
sight-seeing crowd had well gathered, they would
have seen the temple traffic at its worst and most
sacrilegious. In the court of the Gentiles, a wide,
tessellated space inclosed with a noble Corinthian
colonnade, the noise of the rabble, the bleating of
sheep brought for sacrifice, must have struck offensively across the solemn associations awakened in
the mind of every devout Jew on first entering the
sacred precinct. Across the open court rose the
sanctuary from its terrace, doors and lintels overlaid
with gold and silver. By the Gate Beautiful they
went up into the court of the Women, a handsome
colonnaded space into which fifteen thousand wor-
shipers could be crowded. Here between the columns

they found the table of the money-changers, little shops, set up along the wall spaces. One can understand how they would have hung together, the Galileans in their brown-and-white burnooses around the tall figure of their prophet, ignored by hurrying priests, elbowed by insolent temple attendants, while the sense of what they saw sank into them. From the language used by Jesus, when at last he could no longer keep silent, it must have been some extortion, some provincial mulcted of his due exchange, some widow overcharged for a pair of doves, that fanned his wrath into action.

The disturbance, whatever it was, could hardly have extended beyond the sanctuary; the money-changers would not have risked a general riot. At the overturning of the first table they would have gathered up their moneys, the vendors of small wares fled, squealing. After all, the man might be a prophet, and the sympathy of the bystanders would have certainly been on his side.

It is reported that Jesus drove out the money-changers with a whip, and from that time, when he was in the temple, would permit none of his following to carry into the temple the implement and sign of his trade, as was the common practice, upon his person.

There is a ribald song still extant about the sons of Annas, who had a bazar within the sanctuary, which shows how Jerusalem went with its tongue in its cheek in respect to the temple management. A more interesting commentary still, is the fact that not a word of all this leaked through to the Roman authorities. Here was the most influential group of Jerusalemites, manhandled and affronted in their own temple, and nothing whatever is heard of the police, no complaint for assault is lodged. It is a commentary on the utter indefensibility of the temple traffic, and the only tribute paid by organized Jewry to the prophetic character of Jesus. In that brief period of hesitation was let slip the occasion to deal with him as an ordinary disturber of public worship. In spite of themselves they were forced to deal with him as a public character.

Deal with him they must, and that speedily. For not only had he driven out the traffic, but he continued to hang about the temple, both that day and the next, supported by his twelve stalwart Galileans, preaching to the people and enforcing by the moral weight of his presence the embargo on everything not consistent with the traditions of the sanctuary. And this while there were perhaps two or three hundred thousand pilgrims in the city waiting to be fleeced. Plainly the man was a nuisance and must be disposed of. They went about it in a manner truly Hebraic.

The first movement was to send a delegation to

inquire by what authority he did these things, knowing that he had no rabbinical certificates, and thinking to discredit him with the public, for Hebraism
is before all else a religion of authority. Jesus coun-
tered with another question.

"The baptism of John, was it from heaven or of
men?"

He had them there, for if they said "Of heaven,"
why, then, had they not believed it? And they dared
not say "of men," lest the multitude who counted
John a prophet, be moved against them. So, neatly
caught between the clefts of their own question,
they withdrew from the first encounter, and in the
mean time Jesus had the ear of the people. He
preached there in the temple, so full of his message
that he snatched it from the very stones which in
wonder they showed him—for the temple had been
forty years in building, and was judged one of the
wonders of the world. He drew from the widow
casting her mite into the box of the treasury; he
lifted up his eyes from Solomon's porch and saw
the tombs of the prophets whitened newly for the
season of the pilgrimage, and found in them the figure of hypocrisy, going smug without and inwardly
full of corruption and dead men's bones.

On the very day of the cleansing of the temple,
while the rumor of it still ran about the pillars of
Solomon's porch, he spoke a parable in which he

quite explicitly stated that publicans and harlots should go into the kingdom before the chief priests and their following. He scored the Pharisees afresh, "devourers of widows' houses, making long prayers for a pretense," seeing in their pious humbug the greatest menace to his teaching. Moving in imminent peril of his life, he moved as freely as among his Galilean hills, preaching in the temple daily and on the Mount of Olives walking between the orchards, discoursing of the kingdom. It was as if he understood that he was now at the end of his ministry, and was concerned merely to draw out and define again its salient teaching. In and out of a dozen brilliant parables flashed the doctrine of the kingdom as a thing to be done, a task set and achieved, a charge to keep. Men believed, and, believing, acted, and in doing were saved . . . "for inasmuch as ye have done it unto the least of these, ye have done it unto me."

That he missed no point of the situation is evident from his appeal to the preaching of John, knowing the Baptist to have had a firmer hold than himself on the popular imagination, and also from the spirit with which he evaded the next trap which they set for him.

Unable, on the one hand, to discredit him with the populace, they sought, on the other, to set him at odds with Pilate. The approach was well calculated on the basis of his being a Galilean, one of that tribe among whom had developed the most invincible opposition to the Roman authority. Now, as one regarding not the person of man, would he or would he not advise them to give tribute to Cæsar? But the answer, "Render unto Cæsar the things that are Cæsar's and to God the things that are God's," left them exactly where they were before, if, in fact, it did not leave them a trifle more discomfited, for he had glanced here at the custom of paying divine honors to emperors, to which they had been a shade too complaisant. Then came the Sadducees mocking, with a question trumped up about a resurrection from the dead—a possibility in which they did not in the least believe—and were answered out of their own Pentateuch in the words of their only prophet, Moses. In this fashion Jesus fenced for time, that he might drive home his message.

But the Pharisees, when they heard how he had reduced the Sadducees to silence, plumed themselves and came asking, "Which is the great commandment?" Only they themselves knew what advantage they hoped for in the answer to such a question; what came neither they nor the world has ever been able wholly to handle. Said Jesus:

"Thou shalt love the Lord thy God with all thy heart and with all thy mind and with all thy strength,

and thy neighbor as thyself.   On these two hang all
the law and the prophets."

Then, suddenly wearied of question which had no
honest query of the heart behind it, he turned on
them with an exegetical problem so exactly in their
own manner and so impossible to answer that it
put an end once for all to that form of inquisition.
Balked in wit, the priestly party turned to the one
instrument which they understood perfectly, money.
With money, somewhere in his defenses they might
find a weakness; seeking for it by means not un-
practised, they found Judas, the only one of the disciples not a Galilean.

§

The compounding of Judas with the agents of
Caiphas is connected by tradition with an incident
that occurred on Wednesday evening at the house
of one Simon, at Bethany, where the Master was
being entertained at supper.   No doubt Judas felt
gulled and disappointed.   Perhaps he had friends in
the city to wag a sly finger at him.   Here they were
at Jerusalem, and no kingdom; here, after nearly
a year of following, still unaccepted, dependent on
the chance hospitality of villagers, they who should
have feasted in kings' houses! Thirty pieces of
silver, about four months' wages, was not much to
one who had expected to sit on one of the twelve
thrones of Israel, and all that they wanted of him

was that he should guide the temple police to his
Master when few or none were by. He could have
had no idea what was really to be done to Jesus,
for the Sanhedrin itself had no notion, and was
hard put to it, once they had taken the prophet, to
find an accusation against him which would be
acceptable to the Roman authorities. And surely
if the man was the Messiah, when the police laid
hands on him he would have to declare himself.
So Judas must have mused inwardly while the supper
went forward and the uninvited, in the friendly
Eastern fashion, edged up to catch some crumbs of
wisdom as they fell from the prophet.

And as he mused came a woman having an ala-
baster box of ointment, very costly, which she poured
upon the head of Jesus. Thus it was done by the
rich to guests of great distinction; but the thrifty
folk of Bethany were shocked at it as an extrava-
gance. How much more virtuous to have sold the
ointment and given the money to the poor! This
is what is called an eminently practical suggestion;
but the practicality of prophets is of another sort.
"Let her alone," said Jesus, "the poor ye have with
ye always . . ." subject to our poor mechanical
pieties. Once for all he ranged himself on the side
of the generous risks of the faith which, having
risked, finds itself set aside for distinguished service.

"Lord," all they who sat with him might have

afterward said, "had we known you were to die, we too would have anointed thee," but it is only of those who, knowing no more than the rest, act freely on the impulse of the spirit, of whom these things are told in memorial. Judas, who is imagined as protesting most, Judas who carried the bag for the twelve, and was no doubt elected to that office because of his eminent practicality, found in the incident the touch of futility which inclined him in the high priest's favor. He may even have thought, as is the way with the practical, that Jesus was prone to be feasted and fussed over, and that he would spur him on to his obvious mission, which was to take possession of Jerusalem and declare the kingdom.

The next day was spent by the little company in retirement among the budding orchards of Olivet, either as a preparation for the Passover or because they understood that the tide of popular interest, which had set in their favor for a day or two, had rolled back in its accustomed channel. They were swept under by it with scarcely a ripple on the surface of the city's festivity. From the walled hilltop came a murmur like a hive; the valleys were tremulous with the bleating of two hundred thousand lambs led up for the Paschal rite. High over all rang the silver trumpets, the chanting choirs, the beat of mystic dances, all the mingled sound of Israel remembering

his God magnificently. Processions choked the
streets, pilgrim parties, Pilate going ceremoniously
to call on visiting sovereignties, and these calling
on the governor again. In the Roman circus under
the wall there were plays and spectacles.

The backward cast of history has warped out of
all proportion the part that was played here by the
man from Nazareth and his twelve. They were, in
fact, completely submerged in the great national
commemoration. But history has not shown us a
more appealing humanness than that of their leader,
yearning in the midst of jeopardy for the hour of
exalted communion with the race that rejected him,
even though to make sure of passing it with his disciples, he put forward the supreme observance by
a day.

"With what great desire," he said, "have I desired to eat this Passover with you." To miss nothing of its full flavor he ventured back within the
sacred precinct, where the arm of his enemies reached
with power, to a room that had been reserved for
him—by tradition in the house of Mark's father.
Here, when the shadow of the temple reached to
Olivet and the seven-branched candlesticks were lit,
he repaired with the twelve to an upper chamber to
keep the immemorial festival of his people.

Of this no single authentic detail is preserved to
us except what is common to the Paschal ritual.

That the nearness of his death and the certainty of being betrayed to it by one of his disciples was foremost in his mind, we gather from what was recalled afterward, and also that this was not understood at the time by any of the disciples, except perhaps Judas. The words reported are unequivocal, but in the light of the subsequent behavior of the disciples we conclude that none of the references to his death had yet the force of an announcement. Still less can we accept the personal turn which was read back into the occasion by Paul of Tarsus. All that is historically admissible is that at some point in the ritualistic meal, either when he lifted the broken bread . . . (*This is the bread of misery which our fathers ate in the land of Egypt*), or when the Cup of Blessing was poured, he said, "As often as ye do this do it in remembrance of me"—that is to say, as often as ye eat the Passover remember me; a natural human suggestion, for he knew that he should not drink of the fruit of the vine again in this fashion. This is as far as history dare go; but there is no reason why the believing heart may not go farther and stoutly assert its right to the symbol of a communion of spirit of which Jesus himself felt the need.

Another incident of this last supper has come down to us only in that second-century record to which reference has been made, but, like the story of the woman taken in adultery, making good its claim by its complete harmony with what he knew both of the man Jesus and his manner of teaching. Somewhere near the end of the ritual he took a towel and girt himself, and, pouring water into a basin, he washed the feet of his disciples. But, Peter protesting, he said, "If I wash thee not, thou hast no part with me." And the impulsive Peter, linking the act with the symbol of cleansing, offered himself, not his feet alone, but his head, his hands also. But the words that followed are explicit enough. "Ye call me lord and master and ye say well, for so I am. If I, then, your lord and master, have washed your feet, ye also ought to wash one another's feet." In such fashion the man from Nazareth completed the round of his teaching;—to forgive, to love, and to serve. "If ye know these things, happy are ye that ye do them."

It was late when the meal was over; Judas had already gone on an errand more than suspected. The others had sung the last of the *Hallel* the solemn and suggestive song of Israel's triumph:

I shall not die but live,

he sang, who was so near dissolution,

And show forth the works of the Lord.

The hour was upon them.

There is a hint here, in the record of Luke, that
Jesus was not at all certain that he would not be
apprehended before he was out of the city, and that
his motive in returning to the suburbs was to give
to his companions a freedom of action which in
the unfamiliar, crowded streets would not have been
possible.   It goes to show, too, that there was nothing miraculous in his foreknowledge, and that he
drew it largely from his acute perception of character rather than from any mysterious faculty of
prevision.   Except as he gathered it from the
cupidity of Judas and the volatile temperament of
Peter, he really did not know just what was about
to come upon them.   For as much as he understood
he prepared them.   Every man was to take his own
purse and his staff, remembering the time he had
first sent them forth without purse or scrip or shoes
and yet lacking nothing.   Anticipating the possibility of their having to cut their way out of the
city, he advised that any man having two coats
should sell one and buy a sword.   Presently Peter
showed him two, and one of them certainly Peter
carried.

The city hummed with the sounds of festivity—
lamps lit in the upper chambers, family reunions,
hurrying groups of belated pilgrims,—as between two
swords the little company passed out almost under
the temple, whose great gates would be flung open

at midnight, by the north gate into the Valley of
Jehoshaphat and across Kidron.   At this season the
little creek would have been at flood, frothing in its
stony channel.   There was a full, watery moon,
and the smell of sap from the orchards.   Up a little
way from Kidron toward Olivet was a walled garden
called Gethsemane, the place of the oil-press, to
which he had the owner's leave to repair for rest
and privacy.   Here the noise of the city fell off and
there was no sound louder than the babble of the
brook and the soft chafing of boughs.   Taking James
and Peter and John with him, leaving the others at
the gate, Jesus advanced further into the garden,
and when he had charged the three to pray lest they
fall into temptation, he went about a stone's-throw
from them and, kneeling, addressed himself to the
Father.

No doubt the three obeyed the injunction; but
the prayers of simple men are soon done.   They
prayed for their own souls and the speedy coming of
the kingdom; then between waking and dozing they
heard Jesus say, "Abba, Father, all things are possible to Thee; take away this cup from me, . . ." but,
understanding nothing of what troubled him, they
fell presently into the deep sleep of workingmen.

To understand anything of the travail of soul, the
first which possessed Jesus since the Wilderness, we
have to realize how absolutely voluntary was his sur-

render to the occasion which was even now seeking
him through the streets of Jerusalem.   There was
no indictment against him, and no offense except
as he created it by his attack on the temple traffic.
He was now outside the city gates with the eleven
faithful, each with his own scrip at his side and his
staff in his hand, and with at least two swords.
Twenty minutes away in Bethany there were friendly
folk, and all about them the hill country of Judea, as
safe to the hill men of Galilee as his mountain is safe
to the wild goat.   And once back in their own
country, the Sanhedrin would have had no power
over them, and, so long as they kept to that district,
no use for them.   There Jesus might have lived,
teaching and healing a few, and, provided he committed no overt act against the political organization
or the business interests of his time, esteemed a holy
man and dying at last in the odor of sanctity.
Nothing that we know of Jesus, however, permits
us to think that he ever contemplated such an
alternative.   Once for all he had committed himself
to the venture of a rational faith.   He had prayed
that death might be turned aside, but not that he
himself should turn aside from it.   What distinguished him from all other Treaders of the Way was
the close correspondence between his will and his
perception, so that he is seen to move forward in
his appointed path with none of the fumblings and

hesitancies of lesser men. He had none of the feeling of moral helplessness which characterizes re-
formers of our time. It is too much even to say
that he chose, except as the soul is thought of as
saving itself alive by continuing in an active state
of choosing; inbreathing, outbreathing. He suffered
as a man the consequences of his instinctive selection,
but there is no evidence that he suffered indecision.
Here in the garden his quick mind outran the occasion and assailed him with the bitterness of be-
trayal, humiliation, and seeming defeat; the sensitive frame worked out the suggestion of physical
anguish. So between waking and sleeping the three
heard him say, "nevertheless not what I will, but
what Thou wilt," and observed that great drops of
sweat stood upon him. All unconsciously they laid
upon him the peculiar burden of the great, to know
themselves even by those on whose account they
accept greatness, wholly uncomprehended. For
when, from what high and unknowable source, help
had at last flowed back to him, he found the three
still sleeping.

"Sleep on," he said, "take your rest; the hour is
come." And a little later, hearing a noise at the
gate: "Rise up, let us go. Behold he that betrayeth me is at hand." While he was yet speaking came Judas with a detachment of the temple
police to arrest him. They found him as by report

the world had come to know him, contained, courte-
ous, ironical.   Said he, "Are ye come out as against
a thief, with swords and staves to take me?"   And
again, as they bound him, "I was daily with you in
the temple teaching and ye took me not."   After
that silence.

§

Too much is always made of the defection of the
twelve, and not enough of the fact that Jesus point-
edly turned his back on them.   In the flurry of the
arrest one had cried out, "Lord, shall we smite with
the sword?" and Peter, without waiting for the injunction, drew his own sword and sliced the ear of
the high priest's servant.   But, "Put up thy sword,"
said the Master, "the cup which my Father hath
given me, shall I not drink it!"   Not only did Jesus
refuse their aid in this crisis, but it is not of record
that he referred to them again, sent for them, left
any message.   To them the Word had been committed; the last thing he could have wished would
be to implicate them in his disaster.   The last thing
they would have thought of would be to act in opposition to his suggestion.   They were children of
the earth, whose instinct in danger is to be still and
to keep on being still.   Not knowing what was best
to be done, they did nothing.   Several of them had
their families with them, whose safety was their first
concern.   Only Peter followed the guard afar off, and

from him and what could be gleaned from the common report, all our account of that night's doings are derived.

The key to the situation is to be found in the fact that Jesus was first taken, not to the high priest who had ordered his arrest, but to the house of that arch-grafter, Annas. The difficulty was that the chief reason why Jesus must be put out of the way—his interference with the temple traffic—nobody dared mention. Evidently not all the Sanhedrin shared or approved of the buying and selling within the sanctuary. Here we have a thoroughly modern situation: a representative body in the main well intentioned, manipulated by a group within the group, whose spring of action was illegitimate profit. Some indictment of Jesus must be found which would not only appeal to the majority of the Sanhedrin, but would look well before the Roman governor. For the Sanhedrin had for some time been deprived of the death sentence; the most they could do would be to represent Jesus as guilty of death by the Jewish law, and to persuade Pilate to fix that penalty. And none so compctent to have that business in hand as the Sadducean Annas. Eminently safe as a churchman, not troubled by particular scruples, wealthy, astute, he was easily the man to get the better of the comparatively honest and tactless Procurator.

What passed between Jesus and the ex-high priest is not known except that Annas sent him bound to Caiphas; where before the hastily summoned Sanhedrin an attempt was made by means of false witnesses to implicate Jesus in a charge of sedition. It was perhaps not the best charge to make before a tribunal hating Rome as the Sanhedrists hated it. Somebody was found who had heard Jesus say something that could be tortured into a threat to overthrow the temple in three days and build it again. This was plainly anarchical, but even here there was no agreement between the witnesses. When all else failed Caiphas made his final cast; no doubt he had been instructed thereto by Annas; possibly he delayed, fearing to invite in the innermost circle of Israel so stirring a declaration. Made before the common people, it would have been answered with a cry, but here in the heart of the priestly aristocracy it struck offensively across every tradition of caste and religion. Said Caiphas, "Art thou the Christ, the son of the living God?"

And Jesus answered, "I am."

Whereupon the high priest rent his garment as was proper to a high priest on hearing a blasphemy.

"What need have ye of further witnesses?" he cried. "What think ye?" And the elders of Israel judged him guilty of death.

The while this was in progress Peter had come

into the open court of the high priest's palace and gleaned what he could among the loafing guard. About cock-crow a maid-servant hanging about for a bit of chaff with the soldiers, looked down from the gallery and saw him warming himself at the charcoal brazier.

"Thou also wast with this man from Nazareth," she cried to him, accusingly, but he denied it and in the very denial gave evidence against himself, for one to whom the broad Galilean dialect was known, insisted, "Surely thy speech betrayeth thee." And Peter, thinking of nothing, perhaps, but how he could keep on hanging about until he learned what was taking place behind the high palace windows, began to curse and swear, saying, "I know not the man." Hardly had he finished speaking when far down the Tyropœon a cock crew shrilly. Then Peter remembered how the evening before Jesus had said to him in the very moment of protesting loyalty, "Before the cock crow thou shalt deny me," and he went away, weeping bitterly.

It was as well for Peter that he missed what was going on within the high priest's apartments at that moment—the spectacle of the chief priests of Israel drawing aside their garments from contamination as they passed, and spitting in the face of a young Jewish working-man who stood bound in the palace of Caiphas. In the interval between this and the

time when it would be possible to go to the Prætorium with the prisoner the guard relieved the chill
morning watch with a crude game played on the
prophet of Nazareth. Blindfolded, they slapped at
him, saying: "Prophesy! Who was it that smote
thee?"

In order that Pilate should rise out of bed at
seven in the morning to hear who blasphemed the
God of the Jews and who regarded Him, some pressure must be brought to bear, for which Annas could
be trusted. It was important to secure both judgment and execution before the news of the arrest
of Jesus had spread in the city, but this was not the
first time the Sanhedrists had had their way in
spite of the Procurator, and if all else failed there
was the well-known capacity of Annas to make
generous loans to his friends in the Prætorium.
Morning found Pilate on the Judgment seat, but
it also found him reluctant. It is even said, with
color of probability, that his reluctance extended to
the point of sending Jesus to Herod whom he hated,
as being a Galilean and therefore out of the Procurator's jurisdiction. But Herod, more than ever
needing the public countenance, and shy of prophets
since his experience with John the Baptist, after he
had satisfied a coarse curiosity about the Galilean,
sent him back again.

The charge brought against Jesus by the San-

hedrists was that he had claimed to be king of the
Jews. There was a measure of guile in this, for on
nothing was Rome so severe as on political offenders,
but it is also probable that it was the only way in
which they could convey to the Roman mind what
was implied in Jesus' announcement that he was the
Messiah. The Christ had always been thought of
as a king and of the Davidic line. One can imagine,
too, a certain Jewish reluctance to have the mys-
teries of their religion pawed over by this Roman
hireling.

The claim, if it had been made, was certainly
seditious, and Pilate had the man scourged for it,
and again he would have let him go. There was a
custom of releasing a prisoner at this season, concerning which and its bearing on the manner of the
death of Jesus there are many nice problems for
scholars, reaching deep into ancient Hebrew practice. It is enough here to state that when the
Procurator suggested that he so release Jesus, the
rabble who heard him, clamored instead for one
Barabbas, a direct-actionist of that time, one who in
a recent insurrection in the city had done killing.

All this took place in the court of the governor's
palace, Pilate speaking from the gallery, for the Jews
would not go into the house of a heathen, lest they
defile themselves for the Passover, for they were
the leading men of Jerusalem and an example to the

citizens. There were present the chief priest, the accusers of Jesus, and certain of their following, together with such of the idle and curious as could be picked up in the streets so early in the morning, knowing little of the affair, but taking their cue from the majority. But among them all, probably no friend of Jesus. That is why it is impossible to say which of the things written, if any, really happened; whether the governor's wife had a dream, whether Pilate washed his hands—a Hebrew custom and not likely to be adopted by a Roman—whether that question, What is truth? was ever asked and went unanswered. Out of all these obscurities but one thing sounds unmistakably, it was the raucous shout of the mob led by the Sanhedrists, crying, "Crucify him! Crucify him!"

"Why, what evil hath he done?" asks the governor, and again, "Crucify him!" And Pilate, weary at last of the whole affair, delivered him to be crucified.

§

Outside the north wall of the city, going out by the Damascus gate, and in plain sight from the longest road that goes over the Bridge, is the place of public execution called Golgotha. Here, about nine of the morning before the feast of the Passover, Jesus was led to be crucified, and with him they crucified two thieves, for it was the custom to reserve one or two executions for festival times as an example. What had happened in the interim belonged to the time and the manner of his transgression; allowing for the formality of the inquiry and for the sending to Herod, the time of his torment must have been mercifully short. It was important to have Jesus out of the way before the terrified and astounded followers could rally to his defense. He went out as other malefactors, bearing his cross, attended by four soldiers and a few of the idle and curious. In front of him was carried a board on which was written his offense—*This is the King of the Jews.* There was a sting in this for the Sanhedrists, over which Pilate chuckled. "Say not," they protested, "this is the king, but that he said he was king."

Said the Roman, "It is written." He was not in a yielding humor.

There was another group in the little company that followed Jesus out of the Damascus gate deserving some mention—a company of the good women of Jerusalem who made it a work of mercy to succor the transgressor. For the code of Moses was at all points merciful; neither crucifixion nor any other lingering death was allowed under it. In pursuance of their custom, these came now offering Jesus the solace of their weeping. On the cross they offered him wine to drink mixed with hyssop for the deadening of his pains, and though he would not take it, it was the sole relieving incident.

As the day wore three or four of the women of Galilee who had come up to Jerusalem in his company came stealing by the hill path from Olivet and, standing some distance off, observed what was done to him. The soldiers sat on the ground and diced for his garments. The crowd grew and thinned and grew again, for was he not accounted a prophet from whom even in extremity wonders might be expected? Smoke of sacrifice streamed out like a banner over Mount Moriah; clearly they heard the sonorous chant of the Levites and the windy trumpets. All up the hills of Judea showed the pale, silvered green of olives and the almond-orchards turning rosy. Now and then out of the crowd some one reviled him, saying, "He saved others, himself he cannot save." Toward the middle of the afternoon one of his poor, tortured companions cried out in agony, "If thou be the Christ save thyself and us." But the other, "Remember me when thou comest into thy kingdom." And "This day shalt thou be with me in Paradise," said Jesus. So it is reported, but neither they that had heard nor they that wrote it were of the prophet's following.

About the ninth hour, at the time when the Paschal lamb should be slain as an expiation for all Israel, the strained frame yielded a moment to unendurable anguish.   He cried out with a loud voice, "My God, my God, why hast thou forsaken me!" and almost immediately those nearest heard him say, "I thirst." But when one more compassionate would have offered him on a sponge the sour wine of the soldiers, there were others who, mistaking the Aramaic words "Eloi, Eloi" for the name of the prophet, said, "Wait, let us see whether Elias will take him," for they were disappointed that there was yet no miracle.   And while they waited, with a great cry he bowed his head and died.

Ordinarily the crucified are three or four days dying, but the approach of the Passover made it a defilement, according to the Jewish law, for them to be left hanging there in extremity.   Therefore, about the time the shadow of the temple, stretching eastward, reached to Olivet, the Sanhedrists directed that death should be hastened, as was customary, by the breaking of the victim's legs.   So it was done to the thieves, but when they came to Jesus it was not necessary, for they discovered that the spirit had already left him.

Jesus saith *Unless ye fast to the world ye shall in no wise find the kingdom of God; except ye keep the Sabbath ye shall not see the Father.*

Jesus saith *I stood in the midst of the world and in the flesh I was seen of them, and I found all men drunken, and none found I athirst among them, and my soul grieveth over the sons of men, because they are blind in their heart.*

Jesus saith *Wherever there are . . . and there is one . . . alone, I am with him. Raise the stone and there they shall find me, cleave the wood and there am I also.*

Jesus saith *. . . and the kingdom of heaven is within you, and whosoever shall know himself shall find it . . . (strive therefore) . . . to know yourself and ye shall be aware that ye are the sons of the Father.*

Jesus saith *Everything that is not before thy face and that which is hidden from thee shall be revealed to thee. For there is nothing hidden which shall not be made manifest, nor buried which shall not be raised.*

[New sayings of Jesus from two papyri discovered at Oxyrhyncus, 1897-1903. Translated by Grenfell and Hunt.]

VIII

SOME six or eight weeks after these events, at the time when the feast of the first fruits of the harvest was kept at Jerusalem, the inhabitants of that city were astonished to find Simon Peter preaching Jesus boldly as the Christ, and him risen from the dead. There stood up with him on that occasion about a hundred and twenty true believers, among whom were the eleven—for Judas, when he understood what he had done, went out and hanged himself—together with Mary, the mother of Jesus, and James, his brother, and many who had been added to their company by reason of the rising from the dead which Peter declared to men of all nations, Medes and Elamites, dwellers in Mesopotamia and Cappadocia and Egypt, in the parts of Lybia, strangers of Rome, Jews, and proselytes. This was the Peter who had denied Jesus with oaths in the house of the high priest, who now preached somewhat in this fashion—how that Jesus had been approved of God by many signs and wonders, had been crucified, dead and buried, the third day he arose from the dead and had appeared to

Mary Magdalene, to the eleven, and to a considerable company of the disciples. Unlettered as Peter was, such was the faith and fervor of his preaching that on that same day about three thousand converts were added to the number of believers.

Something had certainly happened to these reticent and easily shaken peasant souls to raise them to the plane of spiritual conviction, from which neither revilings nor martyrdom could dislodge them; *something* which had not only rallied them from the shock of his shameful death, but had clarified and fused the teachings of Jesus as the whole of his living ministry had not done. It had reached out beyond the circle of his personal following and convinced of his absolute Messiahship many who had so far accepted Jesus only as a teacher. This is the first unequivocal mention that we have of the members of Jesus' own family among his followers; all that could be gathered at Jerusalem, filled with the holy spirit and praising God daily.

Unfortunately, no first-hand account of the events which had worked this astounding revolution has come down to us; but something can be made out under the legendizing tendency of the time at which it was finally committed to writing. Separated from the suggestion of the supernatural, with which everything that Jesus did began very quickly to be colored, incidents of the resurrection show an arresting consistency with the occasion and its background.

It had been about three of the afternoon when Jesus bowed his head upon the cross with a great cry, and a little before sunset when, in compliance with the Jewish regulation, the body had been taken down. It had been given, at his own request, into the hands of one Joseph of Arimathea, probably a member of the larger Sanhedrin, one of those who had not consented to the death of Jesus, and in any case a man sufficiently in authority to win such a concession from Pilate. It was now too close to the eve of the Passover to admit of any proper rite of burial, so that the body was merely wrapped in a clean linen cloth saturated with spices, after the Hebrew custom, and laid in a new rock tomb not far from Golgotha. The women of Galilee, who had watched the crucifixion from afar off, followed and marked where it was laid. It lay wrapped in a cloth pungent with aromatic and preservative drugs, with no confining coffin, and about it played the cool airs of the garden. One must consider also the condition of the body, how that it was not broken, and that it had at most the marks of scourging, the nailholes in the hands and feet, and possibly a spear-prick in the side. This is to allow the utmost to tradition. Of such wounds none are necessarily fatal, and the spear-wound does not appear in any but the second-century gospel, where it is related with curious commentary that blood flowed from it; but blood does not flow from dead bodies. It was not invariable in crucifixion that the feet were impaled, but sometimes the hands only. It is to be remembered, also, that the body which lay there in the rocky tomb was that of a well man of great hardihood, a man who at the first turn of the tide of consciousness could have reached out and laid hold on the eternal source of healing. Whether or not we are to believe that the tide did so turn and bore him flooding back to life, there is much in the gospel narrative to give color to such a supposition.

It does not come clear to us as does the story that was afterward told of his birth, pure legend, arched and sculptured into a perfect tabernacle wherein is laid up the choicest treasure of the heart, with kings and shepherds, angel choirs and lowing kine, to signify all that his coming meant to humanity, but lies embedded, as the fact story so often does lie, in all the crossing and contradictory statements of it. It is a story of a thing that was known to a scant score of timid and illiterate folk sojourning in a great city, a thing kept secret on its own account and whispered cautiously from ear to ear in fear of the authorities. Finally, when it was some time past, blazoned as a mystery, and only committed to writing after some forty or fifty years.

Yet still the story preserves the form of veridicity. It begins on the morning of the third day, as soon as it was light, with the women of Galilee stealing forth from Bethany or wherever on Olivet their camp might be, for it is certain that the disciples were not lodged in the city. They came by dew-wet orchard paths beside which here and there sprang the little low green-veined flowers, called stars of Bethlehem. High over them the temple walls began to take the day upon their gilded pinnacles; they heard the clatter at the gates from the guard changing, and the hordes of market gardeners with their donkeys waiting to be let in. They found the garden which is close to Golgotha, and then along the limestone outcrop they followed the line of tombs to the one that they had marked. Accounts differ as to why they came, with what purpose to prepare the body for more ceremonious burial, and what happened when they had come, but agree in this—that they found the rock-cut tomb empty and the grave-cloth lying at one side.

Two of the three went back with this message to the disciples, but Mary Magdalene remained walking and weeping in the garden. And as she walked Jesus spoke to her, but she, thinking it was the gardener—for by this time he had got some sort of garment upon him—said to him:

"Oh, sir, if you know where they have laid him,

tell me that I may take him away." Then he called her by her name:

"Mary!"

"Rabboni," she answered, instinctively, to the familiar tone, and, turning, she knew him. She would have kissed his feet, perhaps, or fingered a fold of his garment to make sure if it were really he or a vision of thin air, but he, sensitive from his wounding, drew back.

"Touch me not," he said, and then, reassuring, "I am *not yet* ascended to my Father." Then he bade her go and say to the disciples he would meet them in a place they knew of in Galilee, and so departed out of her knowledge.

One hears how Peter and John, when the women brought them word, came running and stooped down and looked into the empty tomb, not knowing what to make of it. And the next we hear is that two of his disciples, but not of the twelve, and therefore not so familiar with his countenance, walked from Jerusalem to their home at Emmaus. This would have been about a week later, for so the feast of unleavened bread was prolonged from the day of the Paschal supper; and as they walked they talked of the things which had been done at the Passover. Talking thus, they were accosted by one who inquired of them what manner of communication they had with one another that they should be so sad. And one of them, whose name was Cleophas, answered him with an account of all that had happened, speaking of Jesus as a prophet whom the rulers had condemned to be crucified, "But," said Cleophas, "we trusted that it had been he that should have redeemed Israel."

"O fools," said the stranger, "and slow of heart to believe all the prophets have spoken!" Then he began to show them out of the scriptures how it was necessary that the Messiah should suffer these things, feeling his way like a true Hebrew back by the law and the prophets, star-lighted sayings that shot like meteors across the shames and humiliations of the crucifixion. As he held up the events of the last few days to the familiar scriptures, new meanings came out like secret writing held before a flame, and as he talked the hearts of his companions burned within them. It was twilight when they approached the village and heard the cheerful barking of the dogs and the lowing of cattle in the byres. There, as they drew near to the house of one of them, the dusk falling and the cry of the night-jar shaken out in a shrill spray of sound above the strips of tillage, they urged him to come in to supper and a bed with them. But as he sat at table he blessed the bread, according to a custom which was well known of him, and, putting off the covering from his head, in Hebrew fashion after the blessing, suddenly they knew him.   When he perceived that he was known, and that they spoke neither to him nor to one another for astonishment, he rose and slipped away into the dusk.

We hear of him again when the disciples are met together secretly for fear of the authorities, coming unexpectedly into their midst and saying, "Peace be to you, . . ." for they were affrighted, supposing they had seen a spirit.   "Behold my hands and my feet. . ." he said; "handle me and see, for a spirit hath not flesh and bones."   And while they wondered between joy and amazement, he asked them what food they had;   and when they had offered him broiled fish and honey in the honeycomb, he ate before them, talking the while, as he had to the two at Emmaus, of the relation of prophecy to the things which had happened to him and to them at Jerusalem.   Twice he met with his disciples in this fashion, and the second time he was handled by Thomas, who, being absent on the first occasion, had declared that unless he could lay his finger in the print of the nails he would not believe.

There seems to have been some doubt in the early records whether these meetings with the teacher took place at Jerusalem or in Galilee; but as to the two meetings yet to be mentioned there can be no question.   To Galilee Jesus would naturally have turned;   there he would have been safest from his enemies of the Sanhedrin, and there in the lonely places of the hills, where his earliest revelations had come to him, he could have awaited the leading of the spirit. For though he could find a warrant for what had happened to him in scripture, there is no evidence that Jesus had expected this second term of living, or that he knew, except as it was the will of God, why it had come to him. It was not, as he seems to have realized from the first, that second coming of the apocalypse, in which the social order was to be renewed; it was the fulfilment of prophecy, and for whatever else it was he could wait as he had always waited, without hurrying God, without guessing. That he should have gone about in secret was part of the necessity of the time and occasion, part, too, of his consistent plan to disembarrass his disciples as far as possible from the implication of his presence. Also, simply as he had trusted their love for him, he could hardly at this juncture trust much to their discretion. That he had a refuge in the mountain of which nothing was known to them except that it *was* in the mountain, we have seen, and also that he made plans at times without consulting them. That he should have made his way back to Galilee without their aid is neither new nor strange in his dealing with them; in view of his extraordinary spiritual resources it presents few material problems.

To Galilee, then, he seems to have gone, and the

disciples each to his own house and calling. The next meeting is every way in the manner to indicate that Jesus waited his final direction in the hills above the lake of Gennesaret, somewhat removed from its most populous border. On a day some weeks after the events of Jerusalem, Peter and the sons of Zebedee went fishing, and with them in the boat were Thomas and Nathaniel of Cana, and two other of the disciples. They went out at even, and all that night they caught nothing, but when it was morning, the fishing-smack standing close in toward the shore, they saw Jesus calling to them from the land and directing them where they should cast in the nets. But when they realized it was the Master, Peter threw his fishing-coat about him, for he had stripped to the labor of casting, and waded in to the shore. Presently came the others, dragging the nets, to discover that Jesus had built a fire, and laid fish to broil on the coals and prepared bread. So they ate and talked together as they must have done so many times in the beginning of his ministry, when the shared, simple meal was all they had among them of the kingdom.

In this fashion the appearances of Jesus after his death are set down, not other than the appearances of his life, except for here and there the legendizing touch. Of his coming and going in secret, mysterious vanishings are made. Mark, who wrote what Peter told him, says simply that he appeared while the disciples were at supper and upbraided them for their unbelief, but John, writing in the second century, says that the door was shut. Mark says that the women at the tomb met a young man there, Matthew makes him an angel, and Luke, writing hearsay only, makes two of him in shining garments. Such a development in forty or fifty years for an event which, even when it happened, was regarded as supernatural, is less than might have been expected. And then, suddenly, on an occasion which all seem to have recognized as final, the appearances stopped.

It seems that there had been a preaching, somewhere in the hills, and that more than the twelve were present. Paul, twenty years after the event, says that there were about five hundred; others mention simply a great company. After the discourse, when he would have left them, those who were nearest to him in affection went a part of the way, and when he had lifted up his hands and blessed them they saw him pass from them toward his chosen place, of which they knew nothing except that they should not see him again in this fashion; and they believed that he had ascended into heaven.

So passed the most singular and appealing character in all history. The spring was at the flood, the barley beginning to head, and anemones bright as blood pricked out the paths. None saw him go but a handful of fishermen and villagers; Tiberius he left upon the seat of Rome and the eagles flying over Jerusalem, not a tax remitted nor a dream realized, not a word of all his revelation written. Even so he went in the same quiet confidence that had sustained him, more completely at one with the purposes of God than any man who has yet believed in Him, and, as we admit, most completely justified.

§

Paul, when he mentions the post-crucifixion appearances of Jesus, says that he appeared also unto Peter. Of this we have no account, though such an interview is plainly indicated. It is indicated in the complete reinstatement of Peter, who denied him, in the confidence of the Master and respect of the other disciples; it is indicated in the authority which was conceded by the twelve to Peter, even stronger in tradition than in the scripture, where evidence of it is not wanting. More than all else it is indicated in the stout conviction of Peter himself that he had seen the Lord. He preached it, was scourged and in prison because of it, he died for it. His faith in the risen Christ made of him, a heavy, blundering, impulsive fisherman, one of the chief apostles, preaching acceptably in the cities of the known world, establishing churches out of hand.

But of this interview Peter says nothing, unless it be indicated in that reference to the manner of his death which he says Jesus foretold him. And John Mark, who wrote all that he could remember of what Peter told him, says nothing, or at least nothing that has come down to us, for it is agreed that the story of Mark has been cut off at the point where the women returning from the empty tomb were afraid to speak of what they had seen. It has been suggested that the true ending of Mark was replaced by a later version because his account of what Peter told him constituted an admission of the phantasmal character of the appearance, a vision, a hallucination.

But how if it were the other way about, and Mark's story was rejected because it showed all too plainly a man believed to be dead, but found living and as a man disposing his affairs? This would have been the more likely if the young man the women found at the sepulcher had been the same Mark, noticed as standing by at the arrest of Jesus, and fleeing from the officers, leaving in their hands his linen garment, for tradition makes this young man John Mark and no other. The one explanation is as possible as the other; and by the time the book of Mark was written it was not only believed that Jesus rose from the dead, but many other things were believed about him which were no part of his teachings, but were owed to Paul of Tarsus. It was notable that during their lifetime there were several things about which Peter and Paul had the greatest difficulty in coming to agreement. Paul, you may be sure, would have cut off the manuscript of Mark with his own hand if he thought it contradicted in any particular that understanding of the teachings of Jesus which he claims openly to have received, not in the flesh, but in the spirit.

But whatever Peter said and Mark transcribed, there is no question as to what Simon believed on the first occasion of his preaching Jesus risen from the dead. He believed all that we have seen Jesus do and teach; he believed also that he had seen his Master in the flesh, himself and not another. He believed that Jesus was the Christ, and that his crucifixion and resurrection could be shown to be part of the authentic prophecy. He believed that the death and raising from the dead had been permitted both as a witness to the Messianic character of Jesus, and as an assurance to man of a life beyond this life which should belong to those who believed in him. This was important in view of something else which he had come to believe within the last forty or fifty days—namely, that the kingdom might be some time deferred and that many of the disciples, himself among them, should die before it could be inaugurated. But with the certainty that

Jesus was a Christ of the dead who died in the Lord, there was an end of all uneasiness. The last word as to the futility of the kingdoms of this world had been pronounced when they matched themselves against his immortal quality.

It was not alone the conviction that they had seen Jesus risen from the dead, that brought the disciples back to Jerusalem. They came convinced that there were to be no more appearances until the coming with Glory and with Power, so convinced that not the vision of Paul, nor any exigency of the early church, nor any exaltation, gave rise even to the rumor of a later hallucination. They were not expecting visions and hallucinations, but such a veritable likeness as they had seen disappearing up the cloudy mountain. How tender and personal the hope was, even at this distance we can measure. How often they looked out along the hill paths of Bethany, how many times his mother started at a knock on the door! They came together at a set time and place, too consistent not to have been conformable to instructions received after the event which had shattered their earlier expectation. Jesus going from them, had known what no man has with such certainty known since, not only the hour in which his passage from the life of the flesh to the life of the spirit was to be effected, but the sure way to reach back in the spirit, to the spirits of those he had loved and left.

They came back, then, about a hundred and

twenty of them, at the time of Pentecost; more than
had actually accompanied Jesus on his first journey in
the flesh. They came because they had somehow been
convinced that there were to be no more appearances,
and that at Jerusalem they were to wait for a baptism of that spirit which was in Jesus.   For they had
said to him on one of the occasions of their being
together after the crucifixion, "Lord, wilt thou at
this time restore again the kingdom of Israel?"
And he had answered them:

"It is not for you to know times and seasons . . .
but ye shall receive power after the holy ghost has
come upon you . . . and ye shall be witnesses unto
me both in Jerusalem and in all Judea and in Samaria and unto the uttermost parts of the earth."

In pursuance of this parting instruction they had
come together, and finding a warrant for it in the
book of Psalms,—for Jesus had evidently not instructed them on this point,—they chose another of
their number, one Matthias, to be numbered with
the eleven in the place of Judas, as a witness of the
resurrection. Thus having done what they could
to perfect the form of organization which Jesus
initiated, they were all with one accord in one place,
praying and waiting. And suddenly, as with the
sound of a mighty wind from heaven, the Holy
Ghost was upon the company, and like unto a tongue
of fire it dwelt upon each of them. Whoever, in

whatever cause, has received the illumination of the spirit will well know that sense of wind and fire with which it confirms its coming. Descending on these plain villagers and fisherfolk, it lifted them to the most stupendous spiritual undertaking of all history.

No way is hard where there is a simple heart.
Nor is there any wound where the thoughts are
    upright.
Nor is there any storm in the depth of illuminated
    thought.

Where one is surrounded on every side by beauty,
    there is nothing that is divided:
The likeness of that which is below is that which
    is above;
For everything is above; what is below is nothing
    but the imagination of those that are without
    knowledge.

Grace has been revealed for your salvation.
Believe and live and be saved.   Hallelujah!

[Early Christian hymn. Translated by Rendell Harris.]

IX

EVEN in his own age Jesus was recognized as a
mystic—one to whom knowledge comes not by
way of reason and objective sense, but by a faculty
of inknowing. That there is such an inknower at the
back of beyond of the individual mind, every man
has some inkling in experience. To every devout
seeker come certainties on which secretly his soul
rests, irrespective of all rational evidence. To be a
mystic is, then, to be no more than every man is,
except in degree. Degrees in mysticism, as we
measure them, are not so much in the nature of the
thing perceived, as in the completeness with which
it is clarified in the immediate mind of the percipient.
For most men, truth mystically perceived, without
the help of observation and ratiocination, comes
drifting to the surface of the mind the long way of
the subconscious self, taking color from its content
and prepossessions, until scarcely recognizable as
truth. Jesus was a mystic, in whom truth, cog-
nized by the incorruptible, inknowning self, arrived
uncolored in the immediate intelligence. But he was
not the only man to whom such clarification was the
norm of experience. Great artists, great scientists

and philosophers, have had such inner flashes as
they have been willing to spend their lives in eluci-
dating, even to die for, as Jesus died. But Jesus
was the greatest of mystics, for what he perceived
he could tell—in so far as people were able to hear
it—and what he knew, he could do. He had a genius
for mysticism.

To be a genius is to be able to find your way to the
goal without precept or example. It is to be effort-
lessly possessed of the sum of ancestral experience in
a given direction. To be a mystic is to have well
developed within yourself, and to make habitual use
of a faculty which in other men is but slightly indicated. Mystical knowledge may be of any di-
mension and any material; the run of the stock
market or the properties of atoms. But once elucidated in the immediate consciousness, it must stand
the same test that is put to knowledge acquired by
observation and intelligence. It must never be
confounded with what is imagined or fancied. If
mystical knowledge will not "work," if it will not
in the long run, add itself successfully to the at-
tested sum of human knowledge, he who produces
it is no mystic, but a self-deluder.

Mysticism, then, is a way of life; a practice of inknowing either for all the life performance, or for a
particular department of living. A man may be a
mystic in his religion and a fool about his practical

affairs. Or he may be a mystic in his business and fool enough not to have any other religion. Most geniuses are mystics in some sort, but a man may be a mystic without any genius whatever. For genius is not a thing, nor a state of being; it is a process. It is the open path our fathers made, the skill acquired by ancestral experience in special directions. He who has genius goes straight away on that path as a homing pigeon through the pathless air. Many great mystics have become so by instruction, by prayer and fasting and a practice of the presence of God. They have no genius at all; they have only struggle and renunciation and great fumbling toward the goal. But Jesus was a genius. He easily knew and did what other men fumble for and strive. He had a genius for mystically acquired knowledge of God in His relations to man. He was without doubt the greatest mystical genius that ever lived.

§

I have been explicit in this distinction between the genius and the mystic, because I wish it to be taken for more than handsome terms of appraisal. If Jesus were before all else a mystic, then it is in his mystical teaching we must look for the chief part of his gospel, so long, and now so avowedly missed. Inasmuch as he was a genius, it was his genius which betrayed him to the generation to whom that teaching was intrusted. For to the generality, the man of genius has always seemed something other than he intrinsically is—fool, eccentric, poseur, neuropath, god, or possessed of devils. Unless his genius happens to be for the accumulation of goods, in which case he is simply one of the wicked.

The genius of Jesus was for mysticism, and his mysticism was of the inner life of the spirit. This is explicit in his teaching and in every recorded event of his life. It is even more explicit in the life of the Church for as long as the tradition of his real and personal life lasted—that is, for about two hundred years. From the place that knew him, it trickled freshly and the thirsty of soul drank of it, until, reddened by the blood of martyrs, it sank into the dark ages, from which it issued like a fountain in the fifteenth century and is now about to rise again.

How then did it come to be lost?

It was lost at first hand because there was something else in the minds of his disciples that they hoped for, that they looked for him to exemplify and to be. "We trusted," said they of Emmaus, "that it had been he that should have redeemed Israel." This prepossession about the Messiahship and the re-establishment of Jewish autonomy not only colored everything the disciples heard; it colored, as we have seen, much that Jesus said. For Jesus was not only a genius and a mystic; he was a Jew and a small-town man. He was an Aramaic-speaking Jew from Galilee, where there had been free admixture of Greek and Phœnician blood, and there was something in the quality of his genius, a lift and release, suggesting that the path which his genius followed was not all trodden out by the children of Abraham. This variation from the marked character of Jewish genius, more characteristic than that of other, less inbred races, is the sole evidence for such an assumption, for I put no special credence in the stories that arose throughout Jewry some thirty or forty years after his death, either to support or refute a claim that was made for him, of divine parentage, that Joseph was not his father. As preserved in the gospels—though I doubt its authentic connection with the narrative of Luke—the story of his nativity is a lovely myth of what the message of Jesus meant to the simple of heart. Jesus himself never heard of it. But of whatever mixed blood, the background of his thought and his upbringing was wholly Jewish. And he was a small-town man. He had no books but the Law and the Prophets, no words, no figures, no illustrative anecdotes that were not small town in shape and Jewish in color. He was as much bound by these things in the transmission of his message as telegraphy is bound by dots and dashes.

The realm of the mystic is that formless inner life in which there is neither time nor country nor Jew nor Gentile. Truth appearing there, appears divested of all but its own fire, naked even of words. As the inknower translates such truth from level to level of his own consciousness, in its final passage to the minds of other men it crosses a streaked zone of communication, in which more or less modification takes place. Going forward on an urge toward expression, it meets an equal urgency of expectation, already shaped to receive it. That Jesus, even in the intimacy of his personal following, was aware of this perilous passage, perplexed and occasionally a little impatient over it, we can see by the multiplicity of his parables touching the Kingdom; flashing his thought this way and that, in a hope, almost wholly disappointed, to find the precise shape in which his truth should pass to their minds and take fire there. "I have more to say, but you cannot bear it now."

We see the formless sense of obligation toward his message, under which all geniuses rest, take shape at the edge of the zone of communication, as a conviction of Messiahship; and, though he never lost sight of the nature of the Kingdom, he was obliged continually to discuss it in terms of the restoration of Jewish autonomy. There was something in his own mind on that subject, something in his mind as a

Jew, that had no part in his mystical revelation, which added to the confusion of the disciples on this point. But it was never what was in the minds of devout Jews of his time. From the beginning of his talk about it, we can see him undertaking to supplant their concept by his own, taking up the idea in their minds as it was from time to time offered to him, as a man occupied with a task for which the exact implement is wanting accepts a proffered tool, throwing it away again as incompetent to carry his meaning; insisting and insisting . . . "but *I* say unto you, the kingdom is like unto, . . ." though he never succeeded in giving them to understand just what the kingdom was like exactly.

In this manner much of his most illuminative teaching was blurred, and finally lost sight of in the circumstances immediately surrounding his disappearance and his expected return, so immanent that twenty years were allowed to slip by before any well-directed effort was made to gather up his sayings and make a book of them. By this time the best-remembered items were those that bore upon the interpretation which was beginning to be generally accepted, about his death and resurrection. These were, first of all, the sayings which Matthew Levi jotted down in his careful, bookkeeping way; then there was the story which Peter told John Mark, Peter himself being no penman, also a number of other jottings and narratives, some of them possibly contemporaneous, and others so highly mythical that about forty years after his death—at any rate before the fall of Jerusalem—Luke collected and collated the best authenticated into what he evidently intended to be a complete story of Jesus and the rise of the Christian Church. These three gospels are chiefly biographical and definitely related to the belief that the death of Jesus was more important to mankind than his life had been. Finally, a fourth gospel, issuing out of the early part of the second century, which, though I cannot allow it to have been of John's writing, I concede to have been of his remembering, dealing almost wholly with the mystical teaching. Of this character also are the sayings that, while they did not get into the canon of the New Testament, have turned up lately as items of belief and practice in the Church of the first two centuries, like those excerpts from the Oxyrhyncus pamphlets and the early Christian hymn slipped between these chapters . . .

"Unless ye fast to the world ye shall in no wise find the kingdom. . . ."

"Raise the stone, and there they shall find me, cleave the wood, and there am I also."

.   .   .   .   .

Nor is there any wound where the
thoughts are upright

Nor is there any storm in the depth of
illuminated thought.

But even while the hymn was being sung, the
whole direction of thinking about Jesus, what he
was and what he taught, was irretrievably altered by
the teaching of Paul, himself a mystic in his own
fashion, which was not the fashion of Jesus. Paul
was the sort whose knowledge begins at the pe-
riphery of the intelligence, conceived as an idea. When
he went into the closet of the inner self he took the
idea with him and made what he could of it by the
help of the Inknower. What he made with his idea
of Jesus was the Scheme of Christian Salvation. But
Jesus when he had gone in and shut the door, having
brought nothing with him but pure desire, saw
God . . . as do the pure in heart.

§

Jesus saw God as no man before him. He saw
God as the father and man the veritable son; god-
stuff in man, He in us and we in Him. But to the
Jews God was a venerable Jewish gentleman, driv-
ing sharp bargains for salvation, given to choleric
outbursts in which he threw things about, felt better
and repented meltingly, showering benefits on his

favorites. The Jews knew God as a spirit; but to Jesus he was Spirit, whole and at one with Himself. To the Jews, God was a Judge, but to Jesus, God was Love.

This is a concept which, with the help of what we have learned of the constitution of the universe, we now lay hold of intelligently, understanding God as energy; ever present, all penetrating energy, forever and inalienably at harmony with all that is. The Love which Jesus saw as the prevailing trait of Godness, we understand to be that active state of harmonization, that infinite delicate dance of infinitesimals so equilibrated that if any particle falls out of harmony with its instant, there is no place for it to fall but into the harmony of the succeeding instant. I can come no nearer to the Jesus concept of God without using mystical terms such as he used, probably with greater precision than has generally come down to us . . . "where two or three are met together . . . raise the stone . . . cleave the wood . . . there am I also . . . abide in me . . . I am the vine, ye are the branches . . . except ye are in me and I in you. . . ."

Jesus held this concept of God not as a definition, or an idea, but as a state of active awareness, as close to his daily life as the inside of the glove is to the outside. He used it; passing from healing to knowing and from that to foreknowing, and past question, though the accounts of his so doing are cloudy, to a sufficient control over his immediate material supply. But, clearly, he taught that this is a proper use of godness in man, and knew himself not an adept, as is fondly believed, but an apprentice. "Greater things than these shall ye do after me," some of which we have accomplished. If there were ever a moment in his life as a man, when he found himself pushed off from that breast which had nourished him . . . on that cry, Eloi, Eloi! . . . Lo, he had fallen into the lap of God. For, if I read aright the account of his reappearances, he came out of his swound completely in that mind in which his disciples had always found him, completely and knowingly at one with the universal purpose.

Now, though it is clear in the Scriptures that this experience of the indwelling, all-harmonious Spirit, lay back of every act and saying of Jesus, it is equally clear that it was but dimly apprehended through the small-town, Jewish-colored understanding of his disciples. Of his claim to sonship they made a pagan mystery, and of his similar claim for them, a gift. "To them gave he power to *become* the sons of God," by adoption, or later, by redemption, bought by his blood. Of intrinsic sonship the clear concept halted for centuries along the cloudy zone of communication. Of God as love they gathered little more than that God loved them; he was "*like as* a father." They were never sufficiently sure that God loved people who remained outside the church, nor could they quite give up the idea of God as a Judge, though they managed to put off the exercise of that function until the end of the world. Only by a few saints and little children such as Jesus set in their midst to be an examplar to them, has love been lifted past the overtones it strikes out of the human instrument, passion, pride, possessiveness, jealousy.

§

Knowing God as spirit, and love as the mode of his being, and man a partaker of God's nature, Jesus also believed man to be a partaker of God's powers. It is impossible to set aside the evidence that, in relation to the exigencies of his destiny as well as his daily life, Jesus lived at a high level of personal efficiency, and that he undertook to teach his disciples how to attain and sustain such levels for themselves. More than any man before or since, Jesus came teaching that the mystical is the practical. All those high moods which had been the exclusive prerogatives of saints and prophets, he meant to make part of the common use and possession. Mind, Spirit, whatever it is constituting the fundamental alikeness of God and man, he established as the daily instrument, accessible alike to the learned and

the unlearned.   God is as free as air, and heaven as
close at hand in a fishing smack as in Jerusalem.   He
did a healing in the course of an afternoon call, and
forgave sins between the roast and the dessert.   He
drew—though his name people have not yet accepted
it—all the manifestations of the supernatural into
the field of the natural.   "Do me a miracle," said
the fat Herod, when Jesus had been brought before
him bound from Pilate; but Jesus did nothing which
he allowed to be called miracles, nothing which he
did not openly declare to be commonly possible, the
fulfilling of a natural law.   As far as he had proved
God, he declared Him; and he knew and said that
there might be those of his disciples who by the
same means might do greater wonders.

§

It was not because he was a mystic that Jesus left
no succinct account of his own processes, but because he was a genius.   Great mystics of whatever
race and speech have discovered that, after a little
matching of terms, their states are not only com-
municable, but that they preserve an orderly sequence and are to be both taught and learned.   For
most people the process is a long one, requiring both
learning and discipline, prayer, meditation, and inknowing.   But Jesus, being a genius, came so early

and so directly to his understanding that he left no record of the path, probably was scarcely aware at first that the same genius road was not open to his disciples. He had no teacher, never referred to any book or person as having an influence on his spiritual life except John, the only other mystic of his acquaintance. "None greater, no not one," he said, when as a young man he stood at the beginning of his own realization. This, since John seems to us quite of the stripe of minor prophets, may have been the characteristic failure of genius to take its own measure. Or, since they were reported to be cousins, there might have been private communication between them more than appears, warranting such an estimate. But John did no healing, and the healing done by Jesus is too intelligently understood and too negligently described not to have come also in the way of his revelation, the genius way, rather rather than the way of spiritual discipline, as it came to the fifteenth-century saints.

It is possible that if Jesus had come into contact with the group of philosophic Greeks still to be touched at Athens, he might have found among them the habit of discriminating thought, and something of a vocabulary by which the processes of spiritual healing could have been intelligently elucidated, as is being done to-day in psychotherapeutic clinics and psychological laboratories. As it was delivered to a few villagers and fishermen, all that has come down to us is the descriptive gesture. Jesus seemed to have realized both the subconscious engagement of the psyche of the healer with the psyche of the patient, and the part that suggestion plays in securing this engagement. By a single incident of the demoniac that the disciples could not heal, we are made to know that he realized the necessity of a sustained state of mind on the part of the healer, and briefly, that prayer and fasting were the means used to attain that state. He was aware of the irrelevance of healing to his mission, which was to inculcate a "kingdom" in which good health was to flow naturally from a right relation to God. Also, though he left us not a hint as to his technique, he showed himself acquainted with the relation of bodily health to psychic discord, and a normal, human way of dissipating one by resolving the other.

Neither did he leave any technique for inknowing, which he regarded also as normal for all who were willing to accept it as normality. It annoyed him to be continually asked for signs and tokens. Just believe that this is true and act on that belief and you will see that it is so, he said. But the disciples did not want it so easily as that; they hated then, as Christians to-day, to take their religion straight, unclouded by mystery. They were average men to whom genius itself is a mystery, and his genius was

so native to him that he failed to realize the lack of
it in others.   All that he realized was that the disciples were slow of heart, and he suffered the lone-
liness of all great genius in their time, even as beloved among their lovers.

§

It was the mystical life that Jesus admonished his
disciples to lead, as differentiated from the ritualistic,
legalistic life of the devout Jew.

"Know yourselves and we shall be aware that ye
are the sons of the Father" . . . they were to abide
in this consciousness of God within, and it was to be
sufficient unto them in health and fortune, food and
raiment.   There was no limitation to the power of
God in man, and therefore no concept of limitation
was to be allowed to the sincere disciple.   Likewise
there was to be no limitation of obedience to the
inward monitor.   Persecutions, despisings, family
relationships, law and convention were equally to be
set aside at every point in which they impeded the
free play of the divine nature in man.   In his teaching, no such division of personal affairs into spiritual
and practical, as distinguishes most Christians of
today, had any place.

In all or any of the exigencies of human life you
were to ask and you would receive, knock and it

should be opened unto you.   Jesus made no distinction whatever as to the nature of these exigencies,
whether they were of hunger, or disease, or what are
called moral problems.

To Jesus there was no such thing as a moral life
apart from the life of the Spirit.   The more closely
we examine his teaching the more it appears that to
him morals had no value except as witness to the
Spirit, or as aids in maintaining the necessary flu-
ency of spirit.   Good and evil were not to be thought
of as established by general opinion, nor by conformity with the rules of an institution, nor even with
a previous revelation.   Acts, states of mind, were
good or evil only as they helped or hindered that
harmonious interrelation of God and man, within
and without, which is the kingdom of heaven.
Greeds of money and appetites of the flesh, anger and
the natural affections, were to be cut off when and
because they were found to be impeding.   Lust and
pride and anger and hatred and envy were defiling
because they defiled, clouded, the inner life in which
alone God becomes knowledgeable.   They were not
sins, they were simply incumbrances.   There was
but one sin—the refusal to abide in and by the inner
revelation.

Jesus had no moral program.   All the torturing
of the Scriptures for two thousand years, cannot be
made to yield one that will not eventually be found

hampering to the free flow of the Spirit. For his moral teaching is exigent, fragmentary. When a moral question was propounded to him he met it with reference to his mystical teaching. Or he exemplified his mystical teaching with some reference to the moral situation of his hearers. In no single instance did he reach forward and specifically anticipate the moral problems that began to beset his disciples within a year or two of his death. To problems such as have become of the utmost moral importance to our time, he remained oblivious; marriage, the family, prostitution, polygamy, war, and slavery. So far as he expressed himself at all, the family was inconsiderable beside the call of the spirit, and marriage a matter of personal disposition. For himself, he did not choose it. Possibly no question was put to him on many of these points because his mystical teaching was sufficiently clear, so that nobody could suppose for a moment that one could abide in the Father and at the same time be a prostitute, or practice any uncleanness. They were chiefly small-town men who gathered around him, respectable villagers with families, and they asked him only such questions as arose in their own experience. When prostitutes and adulteresses were brought before him he found no condemnation for them. "Go," he said, "and sin no more."

For distinctly, Jesus thought of forgiveness as a

function and an obligation of man toward man. God being love, could hardly be thought of as being in that state of alienation toward man, requiring an act to overcome. The act is man's. And this act, the technique of which is modernly to find, is definitely an act of the inner self; nothing so superficial as imposing no punishments upon, or cherishing no resentment toward, the sinner. Forgiveness is an act by which the sin is made to disappear out of the sinner's consciousness, as disease is made to disappear. The words which Jesus used in this connection have been grossly distorted out of their meaning, for "repent" does not even bear the connotation with which it is commonly charged, of an emotional orgy of regret for what one has done. It means a going back to the point of starting and starting over again. This Jesus knew more surely than the modern psycho-analyst knows it, but he did not explain it so convincingly to the men of his time. Like all the great, he was least aware of his greatness at the points which most distinguished him from the generality.

§

For living this mystical, but not mysterious life, there were rewards, not bestowed, but inherent. "All these things shall be added unto you." He had come to bring Life more abundant, breeding freely all the good things of life. Jesus himself, able as he showed himself to do without them, had a simple, unaffected appreciation of good things, suppers, genial social occasions, ointments, perfumes, clothes as good as he could afford—did not the feed and overfed soldiers of the Prætorium dice for them? The important thing to keep in mind was not to allow yourself to become attached to these things, to be able to lay down this pleasant life when the call came and to drink your cup as it was offered. Finally there was the life eternal to be attained by the practice of the Presence of God, *and in no other way.*

The idea of personal immortality had already come into the Jewish thought through the teaching of the Pharisees, thought of, not very explicitly, as contingent on a strict adherence to the law and the preservation of a high moral tone. But by parable after parable, Jesus taught a personal survival contingent on the attainment of a high level of God-consciousness. There is not wanting evidence that he believed that if you attained it in the last spark of life expiring, that would still be enough to get you intact past the shock of death. Jesus could hardly have thought of the God-part of man as dying. In case of failure to carry your personality across, it was reabsorbed, possibly, into its source, but if you would be you, with all your recognizable baggage of personal identity, it could only be by keeping yourself highly charged with the Holy Spirit, the Spirit making for wholeness. "Except ye abide in me ye shall not see the Father."

To his name people it has always been a stumbling block to have survival hang upon the being of something rather than the doing. For all our tithing of mint and cumin shall this thief go in before us? But it is always so much easier to be moral than to be spiritual.

§

Beside the occlusion of the mystical teaching of Jesus, arising out of the ignorance and prepossessions of his time, there was a habit of his, of speaking in the person of the Inknower, singularly misleading. His opening formula, "Verily, verily I say unto you," was easily allowed for by the small-town Jews who heard him, as conformable to the "Thus saith the Lord," of the prophets, but proved confusing to the mixed audience reached only by the written accounts of his life. Neither was it clear to Parthians, Medes, Elamites, dwellers in Mesopotamia and Cappadocia, in Pontus and Asia and Phrygia and Pamphylia, in Egypt and the district of Africa about Cyrene, Romans, Cretans, and Arabs, that in accepting himself as the fulfillment of prophecy, Jesus had not at the same time taken on a claim to divinity. For among the Jews the Messiah was not thought of as having a divine nature, but as divinely appointed.

So, and by such means, but chiefly by Paul of Tarsus, the word was clouded. For Jesus set up no claim to divinity other than he set up on behalf of every other man. And as for the one clear charge to Peter, on which his church was to have been founded as on a rock, it was tragically mishandled. It had come sharply enough on an occasion in which Jesus showed himself almost come to acceptance of his Messiahship, but lacking confirmation, which Peter boldly supplied; as Jesus supposed, out of that inner light in which his own convictions took their rise. "Thou art the Anointed one," said Peter, "the son of the living God."

And "Blessed art thou, Simon," he cried, "for flesh and blood hath not revealed it unto thee, but my father which is in Heaven. . . ." and on this so long-hoped-for capacity which he believed he had discovered in one of his disciples, to discern truth independently of flesh and blood, he proposed to found his church, for only by such discernment may that which is on earth be brought into conformity with that which is above. So possibly Peter understood it, for when Paul came, claiming a revelation as to the death of Jesus, that it was a vicarious sacrifice (which may be only the longer way around

to discovering that it was his life which was vicarious)
—Peter, because he had no revelation of his own,
perhaps, and perhaps because he recognized in Paul's
claim to inward revelation, the preferred way of
Jesus, allowed it.

For God so loved the world that he gave his
only begotten Son,
That every one who trusts in him may not
perish but have eternal life.

The Son can do nothing of himself
Save what he sees the Father doing,
For whatsoever things He does
These the Son does in like manner,
For the Father loves the Son
And shows him everything that he himself
is doing,
And he will show him greater things than
these.

. . . .

For just as the Father raises up the dead
and makes them alive,
So also the Son makes alive whom he wills,
For the Father does not even judge anybody
But has given judgment entirely to the Son.

Take my yoke upon you and learn of me,
For I am meek and lowly in heart. . . .

I am the vine and you are the branches,
He that continues in me and I in him will
bear much fruit,
Because apart from me you can do nothing.

. . . .

If you continue in me, and my teaching
continues in you
You may ask what you will and it will
come to pass for you.

[Mystical sayings of Jesus. Modernly translated and
arranged by H. V. Vedder]

X

HE was a Jew and young. His country lay groaning under the impositions of Tiberius. Images of the Emperor had been carried into the Temple, and the eagles set over the gates of the Holy City. The customs were farmed, provinces milked dry for tribute, whole families sold into slavery for overdue taxes. Herod played into the hand of Rome. Even if the young Jew, Joshua Josephson, rapt in his personal revelation, could have avoided being touched by these things, he could not escape their effect on the people around him, who, out of despair of their ineffectualness, had turned to an old dream, fiercely, as men sometimes turn to drink, a dream of a Kingdom of the Jews re-established by direct action from God. First there was to come such a time as this under which the national spirit anguished. Then there was to be a forerunner, a Voice crying in the Wilderness. After that the Messiah, with signs and wonders, the witness of his divine election, restoring all Jewry to a state of static perfection such as only Orientals dream of, not by force of arms or by social science, but by supernormal Power and Glory. It was a consummation not to be achieved by the Jews, but bestowed upon them.   The Great Day of the Lord.   *Come, ye chosen of my Father!*

For this is the secret insufficiency of the Jews that, though they produce many great ones, they have in no wise produced greatness.   To this day they bolster themselves against the consciousness of lack, by an individual overemphasis which has become their name trait in the court of the Gentiles.   To the last, their national consciousness remained tribal rather than civil, never a pattern, but a people, one Jew added to another Jew, and these to all Jewry, of which the spiritual projection of ten thousand is no more than ten; full of loyalty and no lack of courage and high intellect, but never able to crystallize the diamond edge by which the figure of empire is graven.   *Therefore* they dreamed of a society full born, permanently stabilized, in which there should be none hurt, and no more crying, the lamb lying down with the lion.   Of all the things taken over from them by the Christian Church, this proved the most stultifying, this dream of a hand-made Heaven, made by the hand of Jehovah.   So long as the church remained practically Jewish, it was looked for any morning.   But with membership increasingly drawn from peoples who had not this dream in their background, from people who felt able, and were anxious to try, to set up their preferred society with their own hand, the dream was put off century by century until finally, after a thousand years in which nothing of that nature happened, it was put off until after death, from which remote region it still reaches a paralyzing finger. There was a type of supernatural story once popular, in which the ghostly visitant proved itself by the mark of its fingers on an arm or a cheek, which promptly withered. Look well at every effort of organized Christianity to realize itself in social terms, and you will find the withered mark of this dead dream of Israel.

But about A. D. twenty-six or seven, it was not dead. It was the livest thing in Jewry, hugged to the breast of those whose backs were bared to the lash; prayers for it mingled with curses on the tax collector. In Galilee and the parts of Syria, their young men talked of it as, ten years ago, you could hear young Jews on soap boxes talking of the social revolution, convinced, such was the rottenness of the time, that it could not be delayed more than a year or two. Not otherwise was the group of young radicals gathered about Peter, with Andrew, his brother, Simon the Zelot, and some others, when Peter, going down to the ford of Jordan to John's baptism, had his attention drawn to a young man from Nazareth by the prophet's commendation, and followed him. Afterward, in Capurnaum, they be-

gan to be all of one company, all Baptists, full of
hope and faith in John's foretelling, debating noisily,
drinking and thumping the table, calling each other
Sons of Thunder, and such like young absurdities,
until the neighbors complained of them.

In this fashion, Jesus, his own revelation not yet
wholly delivered at the threshold of conscious intelligence, was committed to John's idea of the
Kingdom and his prophecy of immediate fulfillment.
Though it is more than likely that a part of the
apocalyptic speech attributed to him was taken
over directly from John, there is no doubt that even
after he began to preach his own revelation of God-
in-man as the only reality, Jesus expected the consummation of his gospel in true apocalyptic fashion.

Here the nature of his revelation misled him. For
in that ensphered inner self of the mystic, where
truth is made manifest to intelligence, there is no
time but Now. To all great mystics, and that means
to the greatest among all races of men, things are
known and declared, of which, after two or three
centuries, people say, "They were ahead of his
time." By this is meant that the great man from
any place where he happens to arise, sees things that
cannot be seen by the generality of men until they
have rounded several turns of the road. Every man
who has had even a little inknowning, will have
experienced the difficulty of projecting his inward

certainty upon the three-dimensional screen of the average perception, in such a manner that it may assume a true relation to what, for his generation, is reality. Attempting to give his own revelation of immediate indwelling, form and identity, to so place it before his disciples that they should be able to cognize it for themselves, Jesus inevitably placed it in that quarter of their horizon in which they happened to be looking, in the quarter from which the expected restoration of Jewish autonomy should come. Given the conditions with which Jesus was confronted, it was impossible that he should do otherwise than as, to the day of his death, we see him, struggling to make his timeless truth conform in time and place to the profound expectation of his race. Humanly there might have been a hope by so doing not to cut himself off, by refusing the figure of the Kingdom, from contemporaneous comprehension. If he deluded himself in anything, it was in the degree to which his disciples understood him. Never so completely as he liked to feel.

And yet never completely misunderstanding.

That the disciples had his sanction for their expectation of swift and far-reaching social change, is evident from their manner of living after his final disappearance, while they were still in immediate anticipation of another visitation, not as those to whom the Kingdom had come, but *ad interim*. At no time did they claim that the primitive form of communism in which they spent the honeymoon of their expectation, had been laid upon them by Jesus. It was assumed as the expression of a community of interest, and perhaps also of uneasiness. When it had served their brief purpose they were reabsorbed into their background; for though they had a dream and a promise, they had no technique.

Since they were so left, without any directive reference to the political imposition and social insufficiency under which they suffered, it must have been because Jesus himself actually believed in a specific, apocalyptic reorganization of society—or that he found the whole social and political complex a matter of secondary importance. For it is impossible to find in the gospels any ground for believing that Jesus was ever interested in social or political reorganization for its own sake, any more than he was primarily interested in morals. He was interested in the life of God in man. He was interested in society inasmuch as it was made up of the children of God, but he failed to conceive of society as a thing in itself, having its own spiritual form and focus, a group soul, calling for a particular quality of illumination. Here the Jewish strain was uppermost. For with the Jew to this day, social effectiveness stops short of an adequate concept of group mindedness. Jesus did not even go so far in that direction as the Jews who rejected him have gone since, and outline a shape of social fixity which should somehow be made to fulfill the still missing capacity for psychic co-ordination which alone would produce a living social organism. Far from being, as he is occasionally credited with being, the author of Socialism, that modern projection of the hand-made Heaven of the Jews—did not a Jew conceive it?—he could hardly have failed to see in its meticulous fixity of mechanical adjustment the economic counterpart of that Pharisaism against which his doctrine of rebirth in the spirit was pushed out. Whatever the political frame of the Kingdom he looked for, it was at any rate something self-organized from within . . . seed in the ground . . . first the blade, then the ear, after that the full corn in the ear.

It is the practice of Christians, confronted with their failure to deduce from the teachings of Jesus the precise frame of political or economic organization comformable to the spiritual content of those teachings, to insist that a logical working out of them would nevertheless produce the wished-for social counterpart of his personal ideal. But the fact is, we have in every age produced good Christians, and multiplied them on every hand, without producing anything approximating a Christian society. For two thousand years we have launched ourselves on a really magnificent scale, on every conceivable experiment for repeating in terms of the whole, the Jesus pattern, without being able to achieve the indispensable condition of a society that "works," as the spirit of the Father worketh from within outward. We are at the end of all our expedients for creating heaven on earth by legerdemain of the intelligence.

Puritanism and Catholicism are alike, so many turns of the screw in a direction that turns out in the end to lead somewhere else. Charity has come to be looked upon as a positive deterrent. We have prophesied in his name, and in his name cast out devils of graft and corruption, and they have returned bringing seven others. We have said lo, here, and lo, there, and we have not yet understood how the Kingdom of Heaven is where Jesus said it is, in the midst of us. In the midst of the group soul, where, had he been able to conceive society as an entity, he would have been able to find it. For, as far as his concept went in this direction, it was certainly that the ills of society should be healed by means of the God-powers within us. Here and now, and not as the fruit of some distant, indirect political action.

§

Thus we can only account for the lack of social discernment, and the apparent contradictoriness of

such of his teachings as may be taken as of social
significance, by assuming that, so far as his teaching
went in this direction, it was also mystical; though
there is no reason to suppose that he meant it to
appear mysterious. For the mystical is that which
being inwardly perceived, is perceived in advance of
the capacity of man to reduce it to terms of objective
intelligence. This is the mark of the true mystic as
distinguished from the mere mystery monger, that
the mystic knows that what he now sees darkly,
shall yet be seen clearly. If Jesus said love your
neighbor as yourself, he meant not in a Jewish shop-
keeping fashion, measure for measure, not even as
one of yourselves, but in the sense of *being* yourself,
undivided part of the Spirit made manifest as men,
mankind. In this fashion we have scarcely begun to
realize neighborliness as Jesus declared it, though we
move in that direction by understanding that no
part of the social fabric can be diseased, underfed,
illiterate, morally unregenerate, without pulling
down the whole social sum.

When his disciples asked him for a criterion of
personal standing in the new order, the ready-made
order of the Messianic restoration, Jesus said, "Let
him that is greatest among you be the servant of all."
Except to the few along the cutting edge of advanced
civilization, still a mystical saying. Among the
class of social engineers, exponents of what goes by

the name of scientific management, service as the
mainspring of social organization begins to clear
from the threshold of mysticism and take rank
among intelligible, business concepts. But for all the
intricate social necessities of our day, what else is
there to be found in his sayings or in the background
of his mind other than the reflection of a profound,
personal ideal on the environment of a small, homo-
geneous, first-century town?

For he was a small-town man, and the mechanical
construction of human society had no place in his
cognition. His illumination, in so far as it traveled
toward the small-town superscription of his environment, ran true to all revelation of the Occidental
mystics since, a movement of growth in which
struggle is the norm . . . *for I am come to bring
not peace, but a sword.* It was very slowly, as he
moved about the country, that the naïve faith in
which he began his ministry, that the world could be
healed of its social misery as he healed lepers, at a
stroke, gave way to a sense of the task too great, as
he saw it, from any hand but God's. How naïve he
was, the shock sustained by his first sight of the
temple traffic is to show. What happened then was
so well within the Jewish tribal concept of Jehovah
losing his temper and laying about him, upsetting
existing conditions, that the most devout among his
following never thought of concealing this incident